Questions
That Sell

Questions
That Sell

The Powerful Process for Discovering
What Your Customer Really Wants

Paul Cherry

American Management Association

New York • Atlanta • Brussels • Chicago • Mexico City • San Francisco
Shanghai • Tokyo • Toronto • Washington, D.C.

Special discounts on bulk quantities of AMACOM books are available to corporations, professional associations, and other organizations. For details, contact Special Sales Department, AMACOM, a division of American Management Association, 1601 Broadway, New York, NY 10019.
Tel.: 212-903-8316. Fax: 212-903-8083.
Web site: www.amacombooks.org

This publication is designed to provide accurate and authoritative information in regard to the subject matter covered. It is sold with the understanding that the publisher is not engaged in rendering legal, accounting, or other professional service. If legal advice or other expert assistance is required, the services of a competent professional person should be sought.

Library of Congress Cataloging-in-Publication Data

Cherry, Paul.
    Questions that sell : the powerful process for discovering what your customer really wants / Paul Cherry.
        p.   cm.
    Includes index.
    ISBN-10: 0-8144-7339-3 (pbk.)
    ISBN-13: 978-0-8144-7339-9
    1. Selling.   2. Marketing research.   3. Customer relations.   I. Title.

HF5438.25.C485   2006
658.85—dc22

                                                            2005033216

Printing number

20 19 18 17 16

Contents

List of Figures

Questions That Sell

Introduction

DOES THIS SOUND FAMILIAR?

> The world is running at a faster pace than ever before and we as
> salespeople must constantly adapt to new situations. In the present
> climate customers do not want to spend a lot of time building rela-
> tionships with salespeople. They want quick and easy solutions at
> the cheapest price. Technological advances have forever changed
> our world; now that customers can do business with companies all
> over the globe they do not need expert salespeople. Instead, cus-
> tomers can get instant access to information on the Internet or from
> the hordes of salespeople that call them each day. Instead of trying
> to be the customer's friend, you as a salesperson need to cut to the
> chase and offer the best deal or you will lose out every time!

These statements are misguided. The idea that our world is fundamentally
different from the world of 1980 or 1950, or even 1900, is ludicrous. Dale
Carnegie wrote his book *How to Win Friends and Influence People* in 1938
and it is still a staple in bookstores today! We might have different technologies now than we did twenty years ago, but the people we do business with
have not changed. If you do not remember anything else you read in this
book, remember that! People are still people no matter what year it is.

If we look back in history we will see that every generation has believed
that theirs was the one that revolutionized the world. When cars were in-
vented, everyone assumed that life and the relationships that make it up
would be changed forever. (The same is true for electricity, television, air-
planes, and computers.) People believed that automobiles would cause personal relationships to disintegrate as people were free to travel hundreds of

miles away from family and friends. In the end, though, the importance of real relationships has not diminished, and I contend that it never will.

How can I make such a bold statement? I have learned through years of sales and consulting that there are two types of relationships: superficial and substantive. Superficial relationships are characterized by chitchat about the weather, golf, and other neutral topics; these relationships are built on casual exchanges and they lack any real depth. An example of a superficial relationship is when you meet a client who went to the same college as you did. There are a few minutes of shared memories and bonding over this coincidence, but this does not change the way you two do business. The second type of relationship is the substantive relationship, which is characterized by mutual benefit.

I ask salespeople in my seminars to describe the word *relationship*. The usual responses include descriptors such as trust, rapport, honesty, and understanding. Although these are admirable qualities to pursue with prospective clients, they are not what most clients are looking for. When customers are asked to define *relationship* in a business situation, they discuss things such as how a salesperson can bring value to their companies. The Gallup Organization conducted a major study of 250,000 sales professionals, the results of which were published in the book *Discover Your Sales Strengths: How the World's Greatest Salespeople Develop Winning Careers* by Benson Smith and Tony Rutigliano. They found that there was little if any correlation between having good people skills and achieving success in selling. I'm not claiming people skills are unimportant in selling—they are. But developing meaningful relationships is more than being friendly. A true business relationship requires you to ascertain a customer's visions, desires, fears, and motivations, and that means asking good questions—questions that engage your customers—and to channel that energy into action.

In this kind of relationship, you as the salesperson are not solely concerned about making money or closing the deal; rather, you want to help the customer in three key ways:

1. **Minimizing the customer's risk.** This is done by eliminating a customer's fears (about spending too much money or buying a product that will malfunction) and making certain that the customer can hold his head up high after purchasing your product for his company. If your customer can sleep well at night because of his dealings with you, he will definitely want to do business with you in the future.

2. **Enhancing the customer's competitive standing.** Customers, like all businesspeople, want ultimately to move ahead. If your product can make them look good in front of their colleagues and serve as a step up the corporate ladder, you will definitely earn a place at the bargaining table.

3. **Achieving the customer's goals.** A salesperson who can provide a solution that will increase profit or decrease cost is irreplaceable. If you can help a customer achieve her dream of taking her company to the next level, you will not only be a salesperson; you will be a true partner.

What do all of the above have in common? In every instance you, as the salesperson, are earning your place and achieving results in order to establish a relationship. Substantive relationships do not appear out of the blue; they are cultivated by hardworking salespeople who understand that the key to achieving success is establishing real value in the eyes of the customer.

For too many years so-called sales experts have been preaching the values of relationships without defining them. Most have argued that salespeople need only to "build rapport, honesty, and trust" in order to further their business ends. These are the characteristics of a friendship, though, and they do not necessarily build a successful sales relationship. Customers do not want to "make friends"; they want to see results and substantive relationships provide those.

Do These Questions Really Work?

As a consultant, I deal mostly with salespeople who sell products and services in the business-to-business market. This means two things: The lessons I am teaching you have been tested and used by thousands of top-earning salespeople in the country. These techniques work, but they take time and effort to learn. If you are looking to create and sustain lasting business relationships with your customers in a way that sets you apart from everyone else in your industry, then you will no doubt benefit greatly from the advice I have to offer.

An excellent salesperson not only must be an expert in her field but also must be willing to embrace the role of "business shrink." What do I mean by "business shrink"? This is someone who can discover the workplace frustrations of a prospective customer. By allowing the prospective client to express his aggravations, a salesperson creates an opportunity in which the client realizes the need for change and seeks out the salesperson to provide a solution. For example, prospective clients often experience difficulties with long hours, an unusually demanding boss, or a vendor that is continually late with deliveries. A salesperson acting as a business shrink can unearth these problems by asking good questions and listening to the answers. Once a salesperson has established her trustworthiness and willingness to listen, prospective clients will feel more at ease revealing their troubles and asking for help.

Why These Questions?

By using these techniques you can make the questions you ask prospective clients more powerful, engaging, and effective. Asking better questions will:

- **Motivate your prospective customers to do the talking.** This requires that you fight your instincts to demonstrate all of the knowledge you have about your product or industry. Instead of boring a prospective customer, get her to open up to you by asking intelligent questions and then listening to her answers. Dale Carnegie, author of *How to Win Friends and Influence People*, states that you can make a more significant impression on another person in ten minutes if you show interest in that person than if you were to spend six months talking about yourself. Asking good questions will make your prospective clients feel important.

- **Differentiate yourself from your competitors.** Studies have shown that 90 percent of seasoned sales professionals do not know how or are afraid to ask good questions. If you learn how to ask good questions, you can automatically set yourself apart from your competition.

- **Demonstrate empathy for your prospective customers.** By establishing yourself as someone who will listen to problems and frustrations, your clients will be eager to talk with you. In our society, we tend to be impatient when discussing problems—we often want to jump to the solutions. Your prospective customers, however, need first to recognize and understand their problems before they will accept their need for assistance. By creating an environment where a customer feels you understand him, you will gain access to information you would otherwise not be privy to.

- **Facilitate a prospective customer's awareness of his needs and help him come to his own conclusions.** Even if it seems clear to you, you cannot tell your prospective customer what his problems are; you need to help him go through the process of discovering for himself the problems and then he will look to you for the solution. Even those prospective customers who are aware of their problems need you to ask good questions in order to bring that pain to the surface. The frustration and other feelings that go along with the problems they have encountered will motivate your prospective customers to act, but only if you pinpoint those concerns by asking good questions.

- **Prompt a prospective customer to recognize the importance of taking action.** Once a prospective customer has uncovered her problems, she will not be hesitant to talk about possible solutions. In fact, she will be eager to discuss how you can help because she will have realized the need to rectify the situation.

- **Discover how a particular company makes a purchasing decision, as well as whom the decision makers are within the company.** All of the questioning techniques you are about to learn will not do you any good if you are talking to the wrong person. By asking good questions and allowing your prospective customers to talk, you will be able to find out who makes the purchasing decisions and how those decisions are made within each particular company. Without this knowledge, all of the relationship-building techniques will be useless.

Bring to the forefront any potential obstacles that might hinder a potential sale. Asking good questions lets you in on the concerns of a prospective customer and his reservations about a purchase.

What Do I Expect from You?

Building real relationships takes time and energy. You should imagine your sales repertoire as a toolbox in which you already have the basics. As you learn the different question types presented in this book, you will be adding new, specialized tools to the existing set. Once you have added these tools, however, you must remember to use them correctly. For example, if you try to remove a screw with a sledgehammer, you will not make much progress and you might ruin the wall while you are at it. Instead of jumping in with the first tool you see, take time to assess the situation and plan the best course of action. If you use the strategies in this book halfheartedly, they will not be effective; the various types of questions need to be carefully arranged and crafted for individual customers and salespeople. Once mastered, that time will be recognized as well spent when you see the results of all your hard work.

I have included exercises in almost every chapter of this book. These exercises will reinforce the practices I share and will allow you to perfect your questioning skills before you use them. It is important that you complete these exercises; otherwise you might not be able to fully grasp the various techniques. Also, it will be exceedingly difficult to digest all of the material in one sitting. I suggest instead that you set aside time to read each chapter at a time and do the appropriate exercises. Then go back and read the chapter once more to ensure that you understand how and when to use that type of question. If you spend the time learning how to use my questions of engagement, I have no doubt that you will succeed beyond your expectations.

What Sorts of Problems Are Addressed in This Book?

All of the problems and hurdles you experience each day as a professional salesperson will be tackled in this book. Here are just some of the most common issues that I discuss in the following chapters:

"I have trouble getting my foot in the door."

"Prospects are in a rush for information but want to wait on taking action."

"Customers say they value service but expect the lowest price."

"I feel like I am wasting too much time on opportunities that go nowhere."

"I get pushed down to deal with non–decision makers."

"I am ready to close the deal and then something comes up at the last minute to screw it up."

"All of the prospective customers I contact say they are not looking for new vendors, but I know they are not happy with what they have now."

"I cannot seem to get the right person."

"My presentations fall on deaf ears."

"They are always telling me they don't have the money to make a purchase right now."

What Will I Find in This Book?

At the most basic level, this book shows you how to ask questions that will get your customers talking. Salespeople are often afraid to let their customers talk. They fear that if a customer takes the conversation in the "wrong" direction, they will lose control and ultimately lose the sale. This could not be further from the truth. Customers have so much information they are just dying to divulge, if only we would give them the chance! When you use the questions of engagement you learn that you can control the direction of the conversation while allowing your customer to have the floor. Research has shown that during typical business interactions customers reveal only 20 percent of what is on their minds; as a salesperson who engages customers, it is your responsibility to get to the other 80 percent. Using my questioning techniques will enable you to unlock that information and in turn present your customers with tailored solutions that go beyond their expectations.

The book begins with a self-evaluation of the typical questions you should ask prospective customers. You will learn by examining those questions that many of them do not produce the desired outcome. After this exercise you will slowly rebuild your repertoire with new types of questions that not only will inspire conversation but also make you stand out from the crowd. All of the question types that I discuss in the book will enable you to communicate better with your customers. They will also serve to help build that business relationship that keeps your customers coming back for more.

At the heart of this book lies my belief that customers overwhelmingly respond to salespeople who express an interest in their businesses and their lives. As I say many times in the book, this does not mean that you should insist on engaging in idle small talk about sports, the weather, or other banal topics. What it does mean is that you need to cultivate real, strong relationships with your customers to make certain that their needs are met. This can happen only when you listen to your customers and really hear what they have to say. At times this might mean simply sitting there while a customer rants about your company's poor service or unreliable delivery. Other times you might have to delve into topics of a personal nature, such as the hopes and dreams of a client. There could also be occasions when you will be privy to internal struggles between a customer and his boss or among various departments within a company. Although these exchanges might be exhausting, this type of business relationship can withstand corporate takeovers and changes in technology. If you are willing to put in the time and effort to cultivate these relationships with your customers, success will be yours.

Boring or Engaging: How Do Your Questions Measure Up?

You probably already have a number of questions you ask your clients during a sales call. Typical questions include:

- What do you know about our company?
- How can we help you?
- Whom are you currently using?
- How long have you been with your current vendor?
- What do you like about your current vendor?
- What do you dislike about your current vendor?
- What's your average volume?
- What are your goals?
- What are you paying now?
- What if I could give you the same/better/similar solution for a cheaper price? Would you be interested?
- Do you have a budget?
- When are you looking to make a change?
- Are you the decision maker?
- Can I put together a proposal for you?

You may feel good about a meeting during which you've asked these questions because you've garnered some useful information about current product usage, specifications, and the likes and dislikes of the prospective customer. But to the customer, the questions you asked were virtually identical to those asked by every other salesperson; there's nothing about your call that differentiated you from the other salespeople the client is considering using.

You benefited from this interaction because you gathered information you did not know before you made the call. The prospective client, however, did not gain anything from this meeting. Most of the call was spent going over information he already knew. So to the client, your questions are boring. They will likely lead to his saying something like: "Why don't you leave me some product literature so I can take time to digest the information and then get back to you?"

Salespeople as Problem Solvers

All salespeople present themselves as problem solvers, yet most never ask clients to vividly describe the problems they are experiencing. Rarely do they ask how the clients themselves are affected by those problems. Without asking these kinds of questions, salespeople do not offer their clients the opportunity to open up and vent their frustrations. Instead of falling into this trap, learn to truly engage your customer.

In truth, any salesperson can gather facts. But the outstanding salesperson ignites the emotions of prospective customers and uncovers what motivates them to act. Unfortunately, most salespeople do not know how to spur people on to action. Either they are afraid to get to the real emotions or they are unclear about what to do once those emotions come to the surface. Although your usual list of questions might garner an adequate amount of information, the questioning techniques presented in the following chapters will ensure that you gain access to *all* of the facts you need in order to make a sale.

Asking engaging questions will not guarantee a positive outcome. Some prospective customers will not yet be ready to admit they need help, and other times a company will not have a genuine need for your service or product. Engaging questions, however, will allow you as a salesperson to see these issues early on and to determine the right course of action for each prospective client.

Exercise 1

Take a moment to write down all of the questions you typically ask during an initial sales call to a prospective customer. Try to come up with as many questions as possible.

Exercise 2

Contact a prospective client and ask some of the questions on your list. Keep track of which questions you ask as well as how much time you spend talking during the call. If you have a tape recorder, consider taping the conversation; this will help you avoid being tempted to overestimate how well you did during the call. Immediately after the call ends, answer the following questions:

1. Which questions did you ask?
2. Approximately how long was the conversation?
3. How much time did you spend talking?
4. Did you find yourself talking more than you meant to?
5. Did your questions serve primarily your needs or the needs of your prospective customer?
6. After this call, do you have a sense of the problems your prospective client is currently facing? If so, what exactly are those problems?
7. Are you aware of the future goals of this prospective client? If so, what is his vision for the future?
8. Do you think you set yourself apart from other salespeople during this conversation? If so, state specifically how you think your questions set you apart from other salespeople in your field.
9. Are you any closer to completing the sale than you were before the call?
10. Do you have a commitment from the prospective client to pursue the next step in the sale? If so, what is it?
11. What do you think the prospective client's impression of you was after the first call?

Now that you have examined your questions, consider honestly how well you think you did. Most likely you found several areas that you need to work on to improve your questioning techniques. Once you have accepted that your questions might need some tweaking, you will need to better understand your audience. Getting into the psyche of your prospective clients will allow you to ask better questions and get higher-quality information. To do this, you need to know where the clients are coming from and what pushes their buttons.

Influences on Customer Behavior

As a sales professional you understand that decisions are rarely, if ever, made by one person. Companies have safeguards and inhibitors to ensure that determinations are not made until all possible factors are considered. While this may be good for companies, it makes your job more difficult. Your prospective customer must report to numerous people, such as bosses, other departments within the company, colleagues on the team, stockholders, and board members, as well as customers who are dependent on the company to deliver a product.

Just like you, your prospective customers are motivated to improve their standard of living, to upgrade their position in the company, and to achieve the recognition they deserve. You will have success building a relationship with your potential customers only when you can get into their world and identify the forces at work in their lives. Figure 1-1 illustrates the different factors prospective customers must deal with when making a decision about whether or not to do business with you.

Who are all of these people shown in Figure 1-1? The category of "internal customers" includes bosses, board members, colleagues, and coworkers in other divisions. Internal customers set limits for how much money your prospective client can spend and may even erect obstacles to block the completion of a sale. Internal customers have their own agendas—agendas that you need to learn about as soon as possible in the course of the sale. Many times these agendas conflict with each other and lead to disputes among workers in the same company. If you can uncover the motivations and concerns of your prospective client's internal customers, you will be able to diffuse the situation and move on with the sale. "External customers" include those who do business with your prospective client. These are the people whom your client wants to satisfy, and therefore you should try to gain as much information about external customers as you can in order to better understand what drives your prospective customer. A prospective

FIGURE 1-1. Factors affecting the customer's decision to buy.

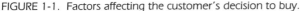

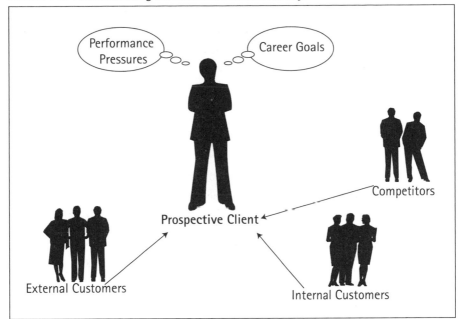

customer who has managerial or senior-level responsibilities will definitely be more eager to learn how your solutions could help in dealings with external customers.

The people you call on are also concerned with the actions of their competitors. Depending on the position of your prospective customers, excelling beyond the level of competitors will be anywhere from a minor concern to their top priority. For example, if you are at a meeting with the president of a company, obviously being competitive is an extremely important item on her list; she will certainly want to differentiate her company from the competition. When discussing software with the head of information technology, however, the actions of his competitors may not even cross his mind. Either way, it is important for you as a salesperson to discover to what degree internal customers, external customers, and competitors influence the decisions of your prospective clients.

Another factor influencing a prospective client's actions is "career goals" and other personal motivations. There's the supervisor who wants to become a vice president, and the president who wants to take his national company to international levels—all of your prospective clients have visions and dreams for themselves. By carefully unlocking those desires, you can present yourself as a "solution provider"—someone who can assist them in achieving their goals.

One final influence on prospective customers is the "performance pressures" they feel on the job every day. These include issues of profits, losses, and costs of production and they can dictate the day-to-day lives of many working people. A salesperson who identifies these pressures can appeal to the needs of prospective customers to meet their budgets, generate more revenues, and reduce costs.

*   *   *

The tools presented in this book will enable you to put together engaging questions. From now on you will be asking your prospective customers fewer questions and getting more information of a higher quality. These techniques will help you set yourself apart from the other salespeople in your field. Once you have finished reading this book, you will have acquired all the skills you need to craft a new set of questions, tailored to your industry and guaranteed to earn the rapport and respect of many more customers.

Getting to Know
Prospective Clients

DEVELOPING ANY RELATIONSHIP is a process, something that takes time and effort. Trying to force or manipulate a relationship into a specific time frame can backfire and cause one or both of the parties involved to leave the relationship. This is true for business relationships as well as personal relationships. In order to cultivate trust and success, as a salesperson you need to invest time in the process by asking the right questions of your clients and prospective clients. Just as important as asking questions, however, is being patient and listening to the rich information that comes your way in the form of answers. Doing so will instill confidence and trust in the prospective clients, the foundation upon which to build powerful business relationships. In this chapter, you will learn about the vital areas to explore when getting to know your clients.

Preparation

Putting together a list of questions before the sales call is essential. That's because your strategy begins with determining what information you need. Before meeting with a prospective client, you should always do your homework. For example, you can access some of the popular search engines, such as Google, Yahoo! or MSN, to gather personal and business profiles on prospective clients. You should also consider accessing business directories online, such as Hoovers, Dun & Bradstreet, Leadership Library, Reference

USA, Corptech, Datamonitor, Mergent, and Plunkett Research. These are good resources to understand a company's ranking in its industry, its financial strength, its executives and their backgrounds, industry trends, competitors, and customer base. The more detailed information you can compile, the more personalized your questions can be.

What if the prospect contacted you? If so, prepare questions to find out what prompted his interest and what is on his mind. Is it a pressing matter, an idea he is just kicking around, or simply a tactic to keep his current vendor honest?

The First Meeting

You want to make a great first impression, so what should you do in the first few minutes of the meeting? Do you jump right into questioning if the prospect knows little if anything about you? How do you provide some background on your company without falling into the trap of doing a sales pitch? These are important questions.

When it comes to building rapport with a prospect, you want to build credibility quickly and set the stage. Otherwise the prospect may ask himself, "Why am I wasting my time with you?" Below is a two-step process to get the meeting going so you can easily transition to the questioning stage and get the prospect to open up:

1. Introductions and pleasantries
2. Purpose of your meeting

Step two is when you give your sixty-second (less is even better) sound bite. Some call it the "elevator speech" because you have a short window to catch a prospect's attention before she decides whether she wants to continue dialogue or not.

How do you condense all that sales information in your brain into a sixty-second commercial that will leave your prospect wanting to hear more? Spend the first eight seconds explaining briefly what your company does or highlighting a specialty that gets the prospect's attention. Then introduce a recent client success story. Prospects relate to stories. Best of all, stories connect with a prospect's emotions. Just make sure that the story is relevant, specific, short, and results oriented (that is, in dollars, percentages, or numbers).

Here is an example of a beginning:

Salesperson: Hi, I'm Paul Cherry [shaking hands as I introduce myself], with Performance Based Results. [A few pleasantries are exchanged, and then I transition into the following.] Before we get started, would it be helpful if I spend sixty seconds on exactly who we are and what we do?

Prospect: Sure, go right ahead.

Salesperson: Performance Based Results is a sales training company. Having worked with more than 1,200 organizations, our goal is to help companies improve their bottom line by maximizing sales performance. To give you an example of how we do this, let me tell you about a recent client well known in the medical device industry [choose the same or similar industry the prospect can relate to] who was frustrated at the lengthy sales cycle of a new product launch, so the client turned to us for help. We put together a plan to coach their sales team on key behaviors linked to specific sales outcomes. After six months, they were able to reduce their sales cycle by 50 percent and they documented over $10 million in revenue that they attributed to our sales training process.

Whether our process would work for you, I don't know. But if it's okay with you, I would like to ask you some questions to better understand your goals so that I can determine if our solutions are a good fit with your objectives. How does that sound?

Brevity is important. A great sound bite speaks results in terms of dollars, numbers, or percentages. It should also hit an emotional desire, such as overcoming failure and/or achieving greater success. A full 98 percent of prospects want one or the other.

Once your sound bite is over, resist the urge to sell. In fact, it's important to pull back on the reigns. Some people call it "reverse psychology," but if you appear anxious to sell, your prospect will pick up on that and get defensive. Plus, you'll sound like every other salesperson trying to push his solution to the client's problem. The key to establishing a relationship is to shift the focus onto the customer and keep that focus on that customer, not on you.

Three Suggestions to Make the First Meeting Go Smoothly

1. **Ease into the conversation with warm-up questions.** Asking about problems at the beginning of the call is risky unless the prospect has

volunteered the information beforehand. Although some salespeople like to ask questions about the weather, sports, hobbies, or a familiar object in the prospect's office, these approaches are overused and they waste your time and your client's time. Warm-up questions are open-ended, broad in scope, and focused on getting the prospect to talk about herself.

Examples of Good Warm-Up Questions

- "How long have you been with this organization? How has your job [or responsibilities] evolved since you started with the company?"
- "What would you say you like most about your work?" "Least?"
- "If your employees [team, coworkers, boss, etc.] were to describe this organization in five words or less, what words would come to mind?" [Listen to the words given and then respond, "The word _____ is a good one; could you elaborate on that for me?"]
- "What would your best customers say are the reasons they enjoy doing business with you?"

Based on the prospect's responses to warm-up questions, you will be able to understand a lot about her interests, personality, beliefs, how she feels about the organization where she works, and the culture of the company in a very short time frame.

2. **Write down the information given to you by your prospective client.** Capture any and all critical information before it escapes your brain. I tend to listen for certain key words and the emotions underlying those words. After you jot those words down, it is much easier to go back and get the prospect to elaborate.

3. **Remove any assumptions you have about this prospect and her problems.** Why do they say new salespeople have beginner's luck? I remember working with a rep who sold high-tech equipment in a complex selling environment. He had been on the job for only six months, yet he closed the biggest deal in the company's history. When he was asked about his secret to success, he admitted that he hardly understood the product. To maintain control of the sales process, he simply asked lots of questions!

Was it beginner's luck? I doubt it. It was more likely that he had no assumptions about his client, her problems, or the product. Instead, his curiosity forced him to ask questions that experienced salespeople would have skipped over because they assumed they already knew the answers.

Salespeople have strong egos—it is what helps them survive the rigors of such a demanding occupation. Yet there is a tendency for people with strong egos to want to talk, to share their thoughts and opinions. Here is a secret: Your customers love to talk just as much as you do! If you can ask questions to get your customers talking, you are much more likely to learn how to attend to their needs.

Questions About the Past

Many salespeople overlook asking questions about the past. Some think that dwelling on what happened last year, or even last month, is irrelevant. They have told me, "You can't change the past, can you? So why bother asking questions about it?" During every sales training session, I ask salespeople to write down all the typical questions they ask on a regular basis, regardless if they are making a first-time sales call or renewing an established relationship. When I collect the responses, without fail, 90 percent of the questions we tally are about the present. Only a few are about the future, and rarely do I collect any about the past. If there is a question about the past, it's usually a warm-up question, such as, "How long have you been with the company?"

Asking questions about the past is a wonderful way to understand your customers' priorities, motives, and behaviors. Imagine that you are interviewing a prospective employee. You would certainly not focus all of your questioning on the present or the future. You would want to know what that prospective employee had done in the past, what she had accomplished, and how she had made her choices. It is the exact same process when you get to know sales prospects: You are interviewing them.

Questions about the past allow you to discover how you can best sell to customers in the future. Questions about the past also help you to unearth your customers' histories and allow you to understand the problems they have encountered in the past, the magnitude and outcome of those problems, the players who were involved, their former or current vendor relationships, and the strength of those relationships, as well as any organizational changes, trends, or competitive threats they have weathered. Everything you need to know about a customer can be found in the past. So why not spend more time there?

Here are some examples of questions you can ask about the past:

- What would you say is different about your organization today from when you started with this company?

- What originally led you to work for this company? What were your expectations when you came on board, and how have they changed since you've been here?

- Since you have been with the company, what have been some of the biggest hurdles you have faced?

- Could you tell me about the changes your department has gone through recently? What challenges or opportunities did those changes create for you?

- As you look back on your career, what has given you the greatest sense of accomplishment?

- What's been your toughest project recently?

- If you could do it over again, what would you do differently?

- What have been some of your likes and dislikes with vendors in the past?

- Can you give me an example of a recent incident in which you had to deal with _____ problem?

- What has been a market trend you've seen in the past few years? What steps did you have to take to adapt to this trend?

Questions to Uncover Problems

How many prospects have you called on who were clueless about the problems they were facing? How many were in a state of complacency about their problems? Or in survival mode? Or hoping that if they could wait it out long enough, the problem would eventually fix itself?

I love finding problems because that means uncovering opportunities. It helps to keep in mind that customers are more motivated to fix their problems than to pursue pleasure. This means that you should dig for problems whenever you can. People are too busy in their everyday lives. They have no time or energy left to step back and assess the actual state they are in because they are caught up in their day-to-day struggles. That is why great salespeople realize the value of becoming trusted business advisers who can help prospects evaluate their current situation and take action before a potential problem erupts.

We all have a preference to stay put. It is human nature. But as salespeople, we need to ask the right questions to open our prospects' minds and get them to think about the risks of staying within their comfort zone. You should never point out a problem to your prospects, however; they should discover it for themselves as they reflect on the answers they give to your questions. Here are some great problem questions to ask:

- Share with me your three biggest challenges. Of these three, which one is the most pressing?
- What problems are you currently experiencing? Why?
- What is causing these problems? Can you give me an example?
- What barriers are in your way?
- What's working? What's not? Why?
- How long have you been experiencing this problem?
- Who else besides you is experiencing this problem?
- Think back to when you originally implemented this process. What were your expectations? What results are you currently getting? What kind of results would you like to get in the future?
- If you could wind back the clock [or wave a magic wand], what would you change?
- Everyone has to deal with change. What's the one change you [department, organization] are encountering? What challenge is this change presenting?
- What are the biggest gripes you hear from your customers? From your internal customers [bosses, peers, subordinates, or other departments]?
- On a scale from 1 to 10, how satisfied are you with your current product/vendor/situation? (Based on the answer, you respond, "You mentioned the number ___. What would you like to see the product/vendor/situation do/deliver/accomplish in order to achieve a 10?")

• What do you see as the biggest hurdle you face in order to meet your objectives? As you evaluate your current situation, where are the biggest areas or opportunities for improvement?

Questions to Disrupt Existing Vendor Relationships

When you ask questions about existing vendor relationships, you have to be careful. You do not want to reinforce the relationship that your prospect has with his current vendor. For example, avoid asking, "What do you like about your current vendor?" Assuming your prospect is fairly satisfied, your prospect could start verbalizing the positive qualities of that relationship, which will undermine *your* efforts to do business. Instead, focus your questions on the criteria your prospect uses in selecting a vendor. Those criteria could be service, delivery, quality, turnaround, or pricing. Once you have uncovered the criteria and what is important to your prospect, start exploring to what degree his expectations are being met, based on those criteria.

Some of my favorite questions to determine how solid the current vendor relationships are the following:

• Would you share with me the ideal qualities you look for in a vendor?

• How does your ideal situation compare with your current situation?

• When you originally chose this vendor, what were your selection criteria? In what ways have your criteria changed as you evaluate your needs today? What would you like to see happen in the future?

• How would you rate your current vendor relationship, on a scale from 1 to 10? (Then, based on the response, ask, "What would have to happen for it to move from a __ to a 10?")

• If you could change one thing about your current vendor, what would it be?

• In what ways can your vendor better align itself with your goals?

Questions to Strengthen Existing Customer Relationships

If you wait for your customers to determine the status of your relationship, you risk hearing about it after they have taken their business elsewhere. Instead, be proactive and monitor your customers by asking them these questions:

- What is it that you value most about doing business with us [me]?
- What do you feel we are [I am] doing right to sustain the business relationship?
- In what ways are we [am I] helping you to achieve your goals?
- In what ways can we [I] improve?
- What changes do we [I] need to make to ensure greater success?
- If you could change one thing about our relationship, what would it be?
- What goals would you like to see us [me] accomplish with you in the next twelve months?
- How can we [I] make your life easier?
- Would you be willing to serve as a reference for my product or company? If so, can you elaborate on what you would say about us? If not, why not?
- What will it take on our [my] part to win the business you are giving to our competition?

Many salespeople refrain from asking these questions. Why? Because they are afraid of the answers. After all, what if customers respond that they are not satisfied? What if they want faster turnarounds, greater discounts, and higher quality? How do you respond? You respond with gratitude and a desire to meet those requests by asking for things in return.

What if your customer wants better pricing? You get him to commit to purchasing greater volume. If your customer wants faster turnaround, price those projects at a premium so that they get the extra attention, commitment, and support that the customer values. Relationships are always two-sided, so do not be afraid to ask what you can do to enhance the relationship while asking for something in return.

What if you already know your service or quality is poor? Then there is no need to ask these questions. Instead, fix the problem. If you fail to do so, your competition will surely do it for you!

Questions About Your Customers' (External) Customers

Surprisingly, not every customer you call on is focused on external customers. Unless your clients have direct contact with external customers, too often you will discover how insensitive to or ignorant they are of their external customers' needs. Under these circumstances, it is likely that internal customers will have greater influence. This makes your job twice as difficult because you need to convince your customers that their external customers are important, and you need to uncover the wants and needs of those external customers. Here are some examples of questions about external customers:

- Who are your most valuable customers?
- Can you give me a profile of your typical client?
- How do your customers measure success as a result of doing business with you?
- What do your customers expect from you as a vendor or supplier?
- How have your customers' expectations changed over the last ten years? The last five years? How do you see those expectations changing in the next three to five years?
- What steps do you take to ensure your customers' needs are met?
- Why do customers buy from you?
- What would your customers say your strengths are as a company?
- What do your customers complain to you about?
- What do customers like most about doing business with your company? What do they like least? What steps are you taking to improve in this area?
- Would you explain the difference between a profitable customer and an unprofitable one?

Be selective to whom you ask these questions. For example, if you asked these questions of a purchasing agent, you would get a blank stare. That's because purchasing has little, if any, interaction with external customers. So, when you ask these questions, make sure they are directed to people who have significant contact with external customers.

The Question of Why

"Why" questions allow you to understand the motives of your customers. Some customers act out of fear, others out of self-interest, and still others out of a desire to increase profits. Being able to uncover motives brings you invaluable insight into how your customers operate. This knowledge then allows you to provide individualized service for your customers.

Getting information on motives is tricky. If you simply ask, "Why?" over and over again, your customers will probably get annoyed or be offended. The examples below give you the opportunity to probe deeper and to better understand what's motivating your customers:

- Tell me, what is prompting your interest in . . . ?
- What's causing this to happen?
- What's driving the need for change?
- What originally led you to this decision?
- Walk me through the steps that led you to this conclusion.
- What do you hope to accomplish?
- Share with me what is motivating your decision to . . . ?
- Why is this important to you?
- What is prompting you to consider taking action?
- What's in it for you to implement this . . . ?
- If you can achieve this result, what will it mean to you?
- If you are not able to achieve this result, what concerns do you have? And how might failing to achieve it personally affect you?

Questions About Company Culture

"Company culture" refers to many things, including how purchasing decisions are made; how the employees feel about the company; what the relationships are between different departments or between headquarters and its subsidiaries; the relationships your contact has with others on her team, with her boss, and with all of the other departments in the company; and how changes are proposed and implemented.

Questions about company culture allow you to become a "fly on the wall" in your customer's boardroom. They give you access to the inner workings of the organization, and they permit you to anticipate problems before they occur.

Remember, employees are competing for a fixed amount of resources within a company. So your plan to overhaul their delivery system, for example, might run into a brick wall if you are not sensitive to the fact that other employees have input into the decision to implement that plan. Here are some examples of questions about company culture:

- Can you walk me through your decision-making process?

- What are the steps that your organization has to take to reach a decision on this type of purchase?

- How do you see the decision-making process going?

- Do you anticipate problems in this decision-making process?

- Tell me your thoughts on this upcoming project. How does your boss feel about it? Your peers? Others on your team? The committee?

- Are there some people within your company who will resist this change?

- How can we tailor this message so everyone sees it as a win instead of a loss?

- How do people feel about working for your company?

- How would people working for your company describe the atmosphere to outsiders?

- Do people working for you resist change or embrace it?

- When making a change, how do you introduce it to your employees?

- What plans does your organization have for cutting costs in the future?

- How do the departments in your company interact?

- Have there been any recent changes in your company's organizational structure?

- Can you tell me about those organizational changes—for example, why the changes were orchestrated? How smoothly were the changes made?

- How would you describe the relationship between your corporate headquarters and your subsidiaries?

- Does one department (for example, marketing, personnel, or research and development) lead the way in innovation?

- Is there a single department that makes more of the company's decisions than any other?

- How does your company deal with issues of staffing?

- Does your company feel challenged by the problem of high turnover?

- How does high turnover affect your profitability?

- How does high turnover affect training costs and hiring costs?

Your Customers' Decision-Making Criteria

Going hand in hand with questions about company culture are questions about the criteria that a company uses to make decisions. If you can get your customers to express the major characteristics that their companies look for in making their decisions, then you can tailor your solution accordingly. These questions will also provide an opportunity for your customers to really think about what is important to their companies when they choose a vendor or service.

Questions about decision-making criteria help customers shift from the "lowest price" mind-set to a discussion of value. Value is unique to each individual, so it is imperative that you ask customers what is important to them. If you can get your customers to articulate value based on their specific needs, then it is much easier to justify your solution as a smarter investment over lower-priced alternatives. Here are some examples of questions about decision-making criteria:

- How do you measure success with a current vendor?

- What alternatives will you be considering?

- Share with me the criteria you use when selecting a . . . .

- How important is price compared to service? Compared to quality? Compared to availability? Compared to "time to market"?

- How important is quality compared to availability?
- When it comes to price, quality, service, delivery, customer support, and ease of use, which is most important to you? Which is least important?
- You mentioned that quality is important to you. Would you share with me your definition of quality?
- Can you give me an example of when your standards for quality were not met?
- Can you rank the criteria you shared with me, from most important to least important?
- Let's assume you are looking at three potential vendors who meet all of your criteria (including price). How would you then make your decision?
- You mentioned that price, quality, and service were three important criteria. What other criteria might be important to you in addition to these three?
- You mentioned that the most important thing for you is price. How does that compare to what engineering (manufacturing, design, production, marketing, fulfillment) thinks is most important?
- When you survey your customers, what criteria do they say are most important to them?
- If you can think back to when you first chose your current product, what were your selection criteria? Based on what you know now, how would those criteria change?
- If you think ahead to three years from now, what do you anticipate will be most important at that time—the initial price of the product? Or the peace of mind knowing that you are getting the necessary support long after a purchase was made?
- Which characteristics of this product are "must haves" for you, and which are optional?
- The changes we have discussed would result in an increase in profits. What would you do with that increase in available funding?
- What alternatives to this problem have you considered?
- You have told me that your company has allocated $___ for this product. How was that amount determined?

- Do you think the allocation of funds is sufficient for the project at hand?
- Based on what I have presented, what do you like most about the proposal?
- Of the areas we have discussed, what might cause you some concern?

Competition and Trends

No business can survive without periodically assessing its competition. Similarly, no business can thrive without a keen awareness of the trends affecting its industry. As you serve your customers, then, you should ask questions about these two very important aspects of business.

These questions will force your customers to focus on the future while critically analyzing their present situation; they will have to ask themselves, "Can I get where I want to go with what I have now?" No matter what the answer, you will have provided them a valuable service by getting them to answer the question. Here are some great questions about competition and trends:

- How do you differentiate yourself from your competitors?
- In the next three years, who do you think will emerge as your biggest threat?
- In the next three years, what do you think your greatest opportunity will be?
- Which of your product's or service's strengths will allow you to continue your success?
- How do you picture the direction of your industry in five years? Ten years?
- What change could cut into your share of the market?
- How does the aging of the baby boomer generation (for example) affect your share of the market? (You could use any applicable trend for this example.)
- How does your company measure progress?
- Are you planning on initiating any integration with other companies?
- How does your company see itself today? How has it changed over the last five years? Where would it like to be in the next five years?

- How does your company approach change?

- What pending legislation (or market conditions, competitive threats, demographic trends, organizational changes, etc.) could change the way you do business?

- What are the market forces you are most concerned about?

- How is your company addressing the competitive pressures of the market?

- What issues do you think your company must address or overcome in order to be more successful? What specific steps or actions will you need to take?

- Describe your goals to increase market share. What's working well for you? What's not?

*   *   *

In this chapter we have discussed many different types of questions that will help you get to know better your customers and their needs. Obviously, you cannot ask a customer (or a prospect) all of these questions, nor should you. It is best to review these questions and choose the ones that work for you. Add them to the questions already in your tool kit of sales techniques. Make them fit your personality and your industry. As long as you cover your bases in terms of question variety, your meetings with clients will be much more productive and meaningful.

Managing Business Opportunities: The Qualifying Process

As a salesperson, you need to be especially vigorous about how you spend your workday. If you devote several hours to writing up a proposal for a prospective customer only to be given the brush-off, no one is going to compensate you for this lost time. Your valuable hours should not be wasted on those who have no interest in pursuing a substantive business relationship. To prevent these time-loss situations from occurring (or at least occurring too much), you need to *qualify* each of your sales opportunities.

Qualifying means determining if the sales opportunity is legitimate or if it is simply a waste of time. As a salesperson, you are probably familiar with the following responses to your inquiries:

"Send me more information."

"Call me back."

"Give me a better price."

"Let me run your ideas by my boss."

"How about I let you bid on a project in the future?"

"Why don't you talk it over with the buyer?"

"Can you give us a demo?"

All of these responses require you as a salesperson to exert effort. Most of them require little or no input on the part of the prospective customer.

Also, the last response could require a trip out of town and/or expending substantial resources (read money and time) without a firm commitment from the prospective customer. These "opportunities" may be no more than a polite way for someone to get you off of the phone.

As a salesperson, you need to remember that people in business are not always forthright with their answers. There are many reasons for this, including:

- They are afraid to say no.
- They do not trust you or do not like you.
- They want to gather information from you in order to renegotiate with their current vendor.
- They anticipate possible problems down the road with their current vendor and want to keep their options open.
- They want to keep you at a distance so that they can maintain power and control.
- They have had a bad experience with a vendor in the past and are afraid to repeat it.
- They are not even aware there is a problem or the potential for one.

Before you start chasing opportunities, listen to how prospective customers respond to your questions. The process of qualifying allows you to answer these questions:

- Is the person politely trying to get you off of the phone and out of his hair?
- Is this someone who really wants to purchase your services, or is he just picking your brain for free ideas?
- Does she want to say no and just does not have the guts?
- Is your timing off? Does the person you are talking with have more pressing problems than the one you are addressing?
- Is the company ready for change?
- Are you talking with the right person?

As I discussed in Chapter 2, "Getting to Know Prospective Clients," you need to prepare a hearty list of questions that you can ask in order to learn more about your customers' needs. But what happens when you ask those questions and you get nowhere? You need a process that will help you determine which customers to pursue and which will only waste your time.

Interpreting Prospective Customers' Answers

Here are some of the things you should be looking for in a prospect's answers before you expend time and energy working on a proposal, making a presentation, or mailing a prospectus.

Can Your Prospect Articulate Her Needs?

Any response to a question about needs should tell you if the prospect has a good working knowledge of the problem and if she has researched possible solutions. If she does not, this may indicate a lack of interest in your service. Or, it may be that you are speaking to the wrong person. If this is the case, your task as the salesperson is to locate the individual who has to deal with the problem and has a vested interest in its being solved. After speaking with the person closest to the problem, you should be able to determine whether a legitimate business opportunity exists.

Is This Need Important?

A prospect's response should inform you whether or not there is a sense of urgency. Does this problem have priority over other needs? Find out why or why not. If the need is not important, the prospect may not feel compelled to pursue your service. How do you determine if a need is important? Ask your prospect a series of questions:

- How important is this issue to you?
- What areas of your business does this affect?
- Can you give me a specific example so that I can really understand?
- In addition to you, who recognizes that this is a major problem?
- What steps have been taken to resolve it?

If your prospect can answer all of these questions with specific details and examples, then you can be sure this is a legitimate opportunity. Without obtaining this critical information, you will need to guard your time and energy with this prospect.

How Does the Prospect Envision the Outcome of Resolving His Matter?

In other words, what would it mean for the prospect to solve his problem? How would correcting a situation enable your prospect to do something that is desired? What you really want to understand is the motivation that will drive your prospect to action. By gaining a better understanding of your prospect's reasons for pursuing your potential solution, you will be better able to create a plan of action.

CAUTION If your prospective customer is unwilling to share his motivation with you by answering your questions, you do not have a legitimate opportunity to pursue. Be careful, though, that your answers are not self-serving. If the prospective customer feels you are being manipulative, he will justifiably feel uncomfortable divulging sensitive information.

Responding to the Answers: The Three-Step Qualifying Process

Use the following three-step process to determine whether or not you have a real sales opportunity. This process will save you time and money and help you avoid frustration.

Agree

Find something in the response to which you can agree. Although this is a pretty basic strategy, you would be surprised how many salespeople cut corners or overlook this step. This is a way to connect with someone on a very basic level, and it gives acknowledgment to the prospect. It also buys you time. But remember not to stop here!

Clarify

After agreeing to some part of the prospective customer's initial statement, get as much detail as possible about the response. Ask one or two questions to gather information about the current situation, the decision-making process within the company, or any concerns the person has about the current vendor.

Legitimize

Determine if the prospect is sincere, or if she is just trying to get rid of you politely. Ask a question that will project your prospective customer into the future and will allow you to make evident any potential obstacles to an agreement.

For example, sometimes prospects would like me to come to their facility to demonstrate a product or to have a meeting in person. I am usually happy to oblige, unless I have to drive more than five hours or hop on a plane and go halfway across the country. In those cases, it becomes a real time-management issue for me. Before I commit to such a trip, I spend significant time on the phone asking the prospect clarifying questions to better understand his needs. I ask, "Let's just assume that I come out to your facility for a day. You're able to pull a group of people together, we do a demo, and everyone really finds value in what we have to offer. What do you see happening next?"

I can get all types of responses, but basically they come down to one of two: (1) "We would 'do' business with you"; or (2) "We would have to run it by our boss, or committee, or corporate . . . or . . . we would have to see if we could get the money . . . or . . . we would have to compare you with our current vendor . . . or . . . we're not really sure." If I get the first response, I am on the next plane. If I get the second response, it feels uncomfortable committing my time and resources because there are obstacles in the way over which I have no control. Before I get on a plane or drive for five hours, I need to find a way to remove those obstacles. Doing so will make it easier to get a commitment once I have met the prospect face-to-face, and it ensures that my time is well spent.

Putting the Process to Work

Now let's look at a few common responses to typical sales inquiries and see how you can use the qualifying process to determine if they are valid.

"Send Me the Information"

Do you often get the response "send me the information" when you call a prospective customer? After you finally get through voice mail and on the phone with an actual person, you are instantly deflated by this response. Or, even worse, you become excited about this opportunity and jump through hoops only to be disappointed by the subsequent lack of commitment. Here are the steps you should be taking when you encounter this response:

Step 1. Agree. Find something within the prospect's reply with which you can agree. In this case, you could say something like, "I would be glad to forward you some information."

Step 2. Clarify. Instead of closing the conversation with the above statement, get some clarification about needs. A good example would be, "So that I get you the right information, what specifically are you looking for?" You could also ask, "What specific information would be of particular interest to you?" Now, the important thing to do is analyze the response. You are looking for the reason someone wants information about your product.

If the prospective client answers a clarification question using one of the following words, then chances are good that this is a genuine opportunity: "We're looking to . . . *achieve* . . . *fix* . . . *solve* . . . *eliminate* . . . *avoid* . . . *secure* . . . *improve.* . . ." Words such as these suggest that this company has already identified its problems and accepted that change is necessary. While the prospective customer explains the problem, you should listen to gain a better understanding of the goals and the solutions that are being sought, and that you can provide.

> **CAUTION** If the prospective customer answers your clarification questions with something like, "Send me whatever you have," this is not a legitimate opportunity. It's a canned response. Instead, look for answers like, "I need information on how this process works in the real world. I have tons of glossy pamphlets on my desk, but I'm looking for ways to reduce our turnover costs . . . by finding the right people and keeping them. . . ."

Step 3. Legitimize. The final step in the qualifying process compels you, as a salesperson, to project your prospective customer into the future so that she can walk you through the decision-making process in her company. One example of your response would be, "I'm going to put together some information that you will receive by this Monday. Will that work with your time frame?" When your prospective customer answers yes, you should follow with something like, "Assuming you need some time to look over the information, when should I call you back to discuss this further?" Now you have a definitive time when you will be following up on this sale.

Then, you proceed with the legitimizing process. An example of what you would say is, "Okay, I will get you the information on Monday. Let us assume for a moment that Friday is here. You have reviewed our information and are pleased with what you see. What do you feel will happen next?" By posing this question, you are creating a scenario that the customer can picture. This gets your prospect thinking critically about your service as well as the process of purchasing it. You will be able to discern from the answer whether or not there is any real interest from this company, or if the prospect is simply trying to get you off of the phone.

Some phrases with which you can begin legitimizing questions include:

"Assuming we can . . ."

"What if . . ."

"Let's just pretend . . ."

"Just suppose . . ."

"Imagine for a moment . . ."

You can then end your legitimizing questions with the phrase, "What do you feel will happen next?" Using these key phrases at the beginning and end of your questions allows you to paint a picture of the event and examines how your prospective client will respond. Another benefit will be to confirm how your prospective customer envisions what it will take to do business with her, as well as any hurdles to clear or objections to overcome. Once you discover those objections, you can use the methods presented in Chapter 8 to resolve them.

Here's one possible scenario:

Salesperson: What do you think will happen after you have reviewed my proposal?

Prospective client: I have no idea. As a matter of fact, I tried it before and it got shot down.

This is not what you want to hear, but it's important to understand the hidden objections of prospective customers. It does not mean that this prospect is a dead end, but the situation is obviously complex and you must make a decision. You can either seek out the true decision maker in this company or walk away from this prospect to focus on more promising opportunities.

Here's another possible scenario:

Salesperson: What do you think will happen after you have reviewed my proposal?

Prospective Client: Well, I would bring you in to meet my boss and our team leader.

Hearing this response should immediately signal that there is interest here. By asking the legitimizing question you learn the next step in the process, as well as who else will be involved in making the decision.

* * *

After you have used the three-step qualifying process to determine that your prospect is legitimate, you can go on to ask more questions. Especially if your prospective customer appears to want to continue the dialogue, you can use this opportunity to gain an unlimited amount of information and secure a commitment for the next step. This strategy saves you time and helps you focus on genuine business opportunities.

Now let us examine some other responses with which you can use the three-step qualifying process.

"I Need to Talk It Over with . . ."

Do you ever feel as if no one wants to make a decision, or that you are always talking to the wrong person in a company? Even though selling to buying groups, boards, or committees is a common scenario today, you must remember that companies do not make decisions—people do. Yet, because of competing interests within an organization, it is often difficult to determine who really has the final say on a purchase and who has the greatest influence during the decision-making process. When you are offered a response such as, "I need to talk it over with Mike," you remember all of these factors and ask the questions that will help you clear up some of the confusion.

Step 1. Agree. Respond to this statement with something like, "Great, I'm happy to hear that you will follow through on that." You need to remember, however, not to end the call there. If you fail to secure a time for that follow-up call or meeting, it is likely that this prospective client may not be motivated to pass your information along to the decision maker.

Step 2. Clarify. Get some more information from your prospective customer. Make sure that you obtain a time frame within which the action will occur, as well as some specifics about the impending interaction.

 If your prospective customer cannot or will not answer your clarifying question, this is not a legitimate business opportunity.

Good Clarifying Questions

"Based on what I have presented to you, what do you like the most?"
"Of the areas we have discussed, what might cause you some concern?"

The most important clarifying question to ask is, "Is this something you are willing to recommend?" If you receive any answer less than an enthusiastic yes, you need to be careful. If this person stands as your representative to others in the company and he is not convinced of your product's worth, then you do not want him to be your sole contact. If you do get a yes, though, you can move on to ask other qualifying questions such as:

"When will you be discussing the proposal with him?"
"Would the three of us be able to get together and address any issues that might come up?"
"What issues do you see as most important to him?"

Step 3. Legitimize. Now that you have a firm time line, ask your prospective customer to imagine with you the next step in the buying process. Ask something such as, "Let us pretend for a minute that you are meeting with your boss [board, committee, team leader, etc.] about this proposal. What exactly will you be sharing with him?"

By getting answers to both the clarifying and the legitimizing questions, you will be able to judge if the prospective customer really does need to consult with another person or if you are simply being politely given the brush-off. These questions will not only reap informative answers but also help you develop a relationship with this prospective customer. Finally, legitimizing questions will allow you to imagine the future of this project and what it will take to secure this deal.

"Call Me Back in Three Months"

Unfortunately, there aren't prospective customers sitting at their desks this very minute waiting for you to call. It should not surprise you, then, that many people are busy when you call them out of the blue. What is important to remember is that you cannot assume anything from this response.

When you hear the answer "call me back in three months," is it possible to determine whether or not the prospective customer is interested in your service? The answer is no. You need to find out more information from this person to evaluate whether you should spend your valuable time calling him again, or if you should cut your losses. Here is how the three steps help you do this:

Step 1. Agree. Whether it's a prospect or a current customer, when you hear, "Call me back at a later date," common sense dictates that you first go along with this request. Although it may sound trivial, make sure that you agree to that request and set a specific time for your return phone call. This minimizes the risk of calling back at a time when the prospect has other commitments or is away from the office. Otherwise, you'll get trapped in voice mail phone tag and might spend another two months calling him back.

Steps 2 & 3. Clarify and legitimize. "Call me back" is a great example in which you do not always have to follow the three-step approach systematically. Responding to "call me back" allows you to combine your clarify and legitimize questions, giving you flexibility on how to engage your prospects.

Though you have agreed to call again, do not end the call. Instead, garner some information to judge the level of interest in your service. Some questions you could ask include:

"So that I can best prepare my follow-up call, what exactly will we be discussing?" [assuming he knows who you are].

"As I plan my next call with you, what will be occurring between now and the next four weeks?" [or the time frame he gave you].

CAUTION "Call me back" is one of the most difficult answers to decipher. Sometimes a prospect might *really* be busy, maybe even in the middle of a crisis, and she has absolutely no time to talk. If you get this response, ask for a specific time to call back. If a prospect is willing to give you that consideration, then there might be a business opportunity. If not, you might want to move on to the next prospect.

You must now quickly evaluate whether or not the answers to your clarifying questions suggest a legitimate business opportunity or a vast black hole in which you would be wasting hours of your time. A prospective customer who can cite specific problems he wants to address, such as low productivity or troubles in human resources, shows that he recognizes the value of your service and should be classified as a legitimate opportunity. His answer would be something like, "When you call me back I would like to discuss how we can streamline our shipping process because we have been losing business owing to delays in this area."

Another legitimate opportunity would involve a situation in which an important person who should be involved in evaluating your proposal is currently on vacation or on a business trip. A prospective client might say, "John, our shipping supervisor, who needs to assist me in making this decision, is traveling, but he will be back within the next few weeks and I would like his input."

Other Options to Clarify and Legitimize

"What do you perceive will be of most interest to John?"

"What key points will you be stressing to him?"

"What concerns do you think John will have?"

After asking any of these questions, follow up with a legitimizing question to evaluate how committed your prospective customer is to your proposal. Some options include "Assuming John likes what he hears, what do you think will happen next?" or "Imagine John is not receptive. How do you think you would respond?" You can have a little fun with this and create your own objections to test how solid the contact's support is for your proposal.

These questions should provide you with enough information to conclude that the call has potential.

Unfortunately, you will not always get to this stage in an initial sales call. There will be many times when a legitimate sales opportunity does not exist. The important thing to remember is that by qualifying each call you will spend time on those prospective clients most likely to do business with you.

"You Really Should Be Talking to Someone Else"

This reply provides a convenient out for many people. By saying, "You really should talk to Jeanine about this," the prospective customer relinquishes responsibility and passes it on to Jeanine. Although there may be some instances when this response represents the truth, many times it is simply another way for the prospect to bow out.

You need to tailor your questions to your audience. For example, imagine you are trying to sell software to the president of a large corporation. You have to engage her on how your product will increase profits, reduce overhead, and improve communications. If you start getting into technical language and differences between operating systems, she might simply delegate the decision to a lower-level purchasing agent. A low-level manager will not be as interested in your long-term promises; rather, this person will most likely be more interested in one factor—price. You will have lost a golden opportunity to deal directly with the senior decision maker and will be left haggling over pennies.

*   *   *

By completing the following exercise, you will have the chance to practice using the three-step qualifying process to determine whether or not you are talking with a genuine prospect.

Exercise 1

Write down (or at least formulate in your head) the three steps you should follow to determine if you have a legitimate business opportunity. *Agree:* The customer says, "You really should be talking to someone else." Write down a sentence that agrees with something the person has said.

Clarify: Find out why the person thinks you should be talking to someone else, and what topic the customer feels this other person will be most interested in discussing. Write down your question.

Legitimize: For the final step, you need to form a legitimizing question. Write down your question.

So, how did you do? At this point, you should have been able to formulate one response and two questions to elicit information from your perspective client. Here are some examples of good answers to the exercise. Check your questions against these samples to ensure that you have internalized the three-step qualifying process:

Answers to Exercise 1

Agree: Your answer should be positive and concise. "Great! I would be happy to talk to Sarah [or whomever the prospective customer mentions].

Clarify: Your answer should probe the possible interest of the company in your service, the prospect's relationship with Sarah, or Sarah's possible interests related to your service. (1) "So that I can prepare for my call with Sarah, what do you think will be of most interest to her?" Or, (2) "I want to be ready for any questions Sarah might have. What do you see as a benefit to changing your current service?" Or, (3) "Based on your past experiences working with Sarah, how do you feel she would react looking at the information about my service?" Or, (4) "So that I will be prepared when I speak to Sarah, what challenges have you experienced with your current service?"

Legitimize: Your answer should include the two parts of the legitimizing question, as well as prompt consideration on the part of the prospective customer. (1) "Let's assume I get through to Sarah and she likes what she hears. What do you see happening next?" Or, (2) "Just pretend for a second that Sarah has read my proposal, can you think of any concerns she might have?"

Exercise 2

Now you are on your own. Supply your solutions to the following dilemma (one you have probably encountered more than once):
Agree: The customer says, "Send me some references."
Clarify: What question would you ask to clarify that answer?
Legitimize: What would you ask to legitimize that answer?

Answers to Exercise 2

Agree: "I would love to give you a list of our references right now!" (This way you keep the conversation going and do not have to waste time and money sending the information. Also, if you agree to forward the information without any further questioning, you will run the risk of not getting a response from that prospect.)
Clarify: (1) "So that I can have you talk to the right people, what specifically would you like to discuss with these individuals?" Or, (2) "I would like to let my references know you will be calling; when do you plan on contacting these references?"
Legitimize: "I am sure that you realize that our references represent our most satisfied customers and will naturally say good things about us. Let us assume that you have talked to them and you like what you hear; what do you feel will happen next?"

Why Qualifying?

Many books on sales and sales techniques put a great burden on the salesperson to close every deal, no matter what. This is a mistake. There will be numerous times when you'll find that there is simply no sale to be had! By pursuing a sale that does not exist, you risk alienating a potential future customer by making yourself a nuisance. Also, you will be spending your valuable time and energy without getting anything in return. This is why the three-step qualifying process is so important. In a matter of a few minutes, and with some well-constructed questions, you will be able to evaluate whether or not a prospect has genuine interest in doing business with you. You will save time and money, not to mention enormous amounts of aggravation on your part as well as the prospective customer's. Furthermore, the answers you will elicit by using this process will provide you with invaluable information about your prospect and her company.

Using these answers will allow you to better prepare any proposal you might submit to this prospect in the future. It will permit you to anticipate the most likely objections your prospect might have, while giving you an opportunity to address them. Figure 3-1 on the following pages is a chart that will allow you to adapt this process for many different situations.

FIGURE 3-1. A quick guide to the three-step qualifying process.

Customer Response	Agree	Clarify	Legitimize	Things to Remember
Send me a quote.	Sure! I would be happy to send you a quote.	What is it that you are hoping to accomplish? OR So that I can best serve you, tell me about your needs.	I will get to work and spend some time considering your needs in order to get you a quote. Let us assume for a minute that we can meet your time frame and needs. What do you see as the next step?	If the customer cannot give you concrete answers about his or her needs or goals, this is probably not a legitimate business opportunity.
Send me some references.	I would love to give you a list of our references right over the phone.	So that I can have you talk to the right people, what specific kind of information would you like to get from these people? OR I want to let my references know that you will be calling. When exactly do you think you will be contacting them?	Now that I have given you a list of references, let us look a little bit into the future. Assume that you have talked to them and are happy with what you hear. What do you anticipate will happen next?	If you simply agree to send references without any follow-up you will most likely not get any feedback from the customer. You will probably send her the information in the mail and then never hear from her again.
You should really be talking to Lou.	Great! I would be happy to talk with Lou in purchasing.	I want to be prepared for my call to Lou. What do you think he will be most interested in discussing?	Pretend that Lou likes what he hears. What do you think will be a next step?	Do not hang up and blindly call Lou without getting more information; otherwise he's likely to brush you off.

Send me the information in the mail.	I would be happy to put together some information for you about my service.	I want to send you the best information tailored to your needs. What exactly are you looking for? OR I have lots of information I could send you. Tell me some of your goals (or worries) so that I can give you only the stuff you would be interested in.	I will gladly send you the packet of information once I put it together. Let's assume you like what you see. What do you think will happen next?	If you spend tons of time and energy into putting together information for this customer without first deciding if she is an authentic opportunity, all you will have done is wasted your time and money.
Call me back.	Sure, I know that you are very busy and I would be happy to call you back.	So that I am prepared the next time we talk, what exactly are you interested in discussing? OR What will be going on in the next few weeks that might affect your needs or goals?	[The clarify and legitimize questions have been combined under "Clarify"]	Many times when someone says, "Call me back," he really means, "Go away." Make sure to get concrete details about the customer's needs to ensure that he is really interested.
I need to talk it over with	Wonderful, I am happy to hear you will do that.	When do you think you will be discussing my proposal with your boss?	What do you anticipate will be of most interest to your boss? OR What concerns might your boss have?	By asking good questions you will learn a lot about the customer, his relationship with his boss, and the company's decision-making process.

Getting Your Customers Talking: Expansion and Comparison Questions

THE VARIOUS TYPES of questions introduced in this and the next three chapters will provide you with a kit of helpful tools to use throughout the selling process. Expansion questions, comparison questions, educational questions, lock-on questions, impact questions, and vision questions will enable you to address the various influences on your prospective customers' reactions. Once you have learned how to formulate these questions, you can introduce them into your repertoire and maximize your business interactions.

Expansion Questions

Among the several types of questions that you should use to engage your prospective customers is the expansion question. This question type develops your basic fact-seeking request into a probing question that elicits more detailed information. Expansion questions allow you to sit back and let the customer do the talking.

Ordinary Questions Transformed into Expansion Questions

- Ordinary: "Who is the decision maker?" "When will you make a decision?" "What is your time frame?"

- Expansion: "Walk me through your company's decision-making process."
  Here one expansion question takes the place of *three* ordinary questions.

- Ordinary: "Are you satisfied with your current system?"
- Expansion: "Share with me your level of satisfaction with your current system."

- Ordinary: "What do you like about your current vendor?"
- Expansion: "Describe for me the qualities you look for when choosing a vendor."

- Ordinary: "Is price important to you?" "Is quality important to you?" "Is service important to you?"
- Expansion: "Explain to me the criteria you use to make a decision." This is another situation in which three questions can be transformed into one question.

Expansion questions should begin with phrases such as:

"Describe for me. . . ."

"Share with me. . . ."

"Explain. . . ."

"Walk me through. . . ."

"Tell me. . . ."

These phrases signal to your prospective customers that you really want to hear what they have to say and you are prompting them to elaborate on their answers. Let us look at a sample conversation using ordinary questions and then one peppered with expansion questions. Mark, a sales professional with ten years' experience, calls on Lisa, a purchasing agent working for National Trucking Corporation. After a few pleasantries about the weather and the holiday season, Mark gets down to business:

Mark: Lisa, who is the decision maker at National Trucking?

Lisa: I am.

Mark: Okay, what is your time frame to make a change?

Lisa: As soon as possible.

Mark: What are your goals?

Lisa: To make more money in less time.

Mark: Can I put together a proposal for you?

Lisa: Fine, send it over.

Post-Game Analysis: It's doubtful Mark closed the sale because he limited himself to asking ordinary questions. A salesperson who asked expansion questions would have gotten more information and gained a better understanding of Lisa's situation. Now let us see what happens when Mark uses a few expansion questions to discover how National Trucking operates and the influences (external customers, internal customers, competitors, career goals, or performance pressures) on Lisa's ability to make a decision.

Mark: Lisa, I was wondering if you could walk me through your company's decision-making process.

Lisa: Well, I would initially review any proposals dealing with a change in vendor. If I think a change is appropriate and I like what I see in the proposal, I would forward my recommendation to the regional supervisor. The regional supervisor, Al, would then look over the information and determine whether or not a new contract would be feasible. After Al approves the move, the next step would be to submit the proposal to our divisional vice president, John Williams. Following John's decision, the company would set up a two-week test to judge initial performance. If all goes well, the next step would be for me to create a purchase order and finalize the sale.

Mark: So, it looks like there are a lot of decision makers in your company. Could you share with me what specific goals you and those involved would like to accomplish by making a change to your current system?

Lisa: Let's see, we have not yet really defined our goals. In fact, we've been experiencing problems for over a year now, so I guess no one is in a real hurry to do anything. I seem to be the only one who realizes there's a problem, because I am the one staying late and trying to fix everything. No one else seems to care but me.

Mark: Wow, it sounds like you have a real problem that no one else has noticed. Based on what you have shared with me, I think you should introduce me to the divisional vice president. I would definitely be able to shed some light on the issue, especially since my company has a proven track record with problems of this nature. When would be a good time for all of us to meet?

Lisa: I will find out and schedule a meeting as soon as possible.

Post-Game Analysis: By using just a few expansion questions, Mark learned a number of valuable things about Lisa and National Trucking. First, he realized that Lisa did not have enough authority to make a final decision about changing vendors, but that any change would have to be initiated by her. Mark also discovered that Lisa was the person in the company really experiencing problems because of the current situation. Once he found this out, he knew she would be an enthusiastic promoter on his behalf because she wanted the situation to be resolved.

*   *   *

Upon learning about the multistep decision-making process, Mark decided he would get Lisa's support and go directly to the top to make his pitch for a new contract. Not only did Mark garner a meeting with a divisional vice president; he gained inside information about the issue at hand as well as how the company usually makes decisions.

When asked ordinary questions, Lisa did not reveal her frustrations and negative feelings about her current situation. If Mark had simply ended the call after the first scenario, his effort would have most likely been futile. Lisa already knew her company had a problem, but she had no confidence that anyone else would recognize the need for change. What would have been Mark's chances for success in that situation? They probably would have been very slim, but he had no way of knowing that unless he engaged the prospective customer. On the other hand, Mark's expansion questions sparked a reaction in Lisa and spurred her on to schedule a meeting with someone empowered to make a decision.

We will return to Mark's situation later, but for now you should be thinking about how to use expansion questions in your professional life.

Exercise 1

Choose four or five of your questions from Exercise 1 in Chapter 1 that begin with either "who," "what," "where," "why," or "when." Then,

> transform those questions into expansion questions (which begin with one of the following phrases: "Describe for me," "Share with me," "Explain," "Walk me through," "Tell me").

Notice that in this exercise I did not tell you to make all of your questions expansion questions. This is because expansion questions, like the other types of questions described in this book, should be used sparingly. After reading about other types of questions, you will be able to go back to your original list and designate which questions should be altered to best suit your professional situation. Once you are comfortable with creating your own expansion questions, you will not need to worry so much about using the suggested phrases. However, I recommend that initially you construct your expansion questions this way in order to remember that the goal is for the customer to do the talking. Once you have embraced that precept, feel free to change the wording to better fit your style.

Comparison Questions

Another type of question in your tool kit should be the comparison question. As you have probably guessed from the name, comparison questions use some variant on the word *compare*, such as *contrast, differ, whether*, or *versus*. Comparison questions are slightly more sophisticated than expansion questions, and they require some more thought; however, the benefits of comparison questions outweigh any time put into creating them. A comparison question can open up several avenues for discussion, including:

- **Time.** Comparison questions can uncover events in the prospective customer's past, as well as what he hopes for in the future. A comparison question can also help you identify those issues that are pressing concerns, as well as how these priorities shift over months and years.

- **Decision Makers.** Comparison questions allow you, as the salesperson, to gain access to the inner workings of the organization and to find out who makes the big decisions. They allow you, as an outsider, to uncover competing or conflicting interests among employees of the company. You can easily find a champion (in the previous case, this would be Lisa) and identify possible pockets of resistance. Comparison questions open up the decision-making process and give you access to the politics within the organization. Being aware of potential political pitfalls can help you prepare a counterargument to any argument that might arise.

- **Competitors.** Comparison questions can stimulate a dialogue with the prospect about the industry; they can lead to information about who is the competition, as well as what aspects of the company need improvement. Especially when you are meeting with higher-level decision makers, their concerns about differentiating the company's products and services in a competitive market are the same concerns you face as a salesperson. Using a comparison question can help customers see that you relate to their situation and might have a solution.

- **Alternative Choices.** Comparison questions can open the door to new solutions for your prospective customers. You can ask questions that illuminate any dissatisfaction they feel with a current product or service and in turn show how your solution can eliminate those problems.

Typical Questions Changed into Comparison Questions

Time Example
- Ordinary: "What are your goals?"
- Comparison: "Share with me what you hope to accomplish in the next twelve months. How does this compare with where you are today?" Or, "Share with me what you hope to accomplish in the next twelve months compared with where you were one year ago."

Alternative Choice Example
- Ordinary: "What do you like about your current system?"
- Comparison: "Describe for me what you like about your current system versus what you do not like."

Decision-Maker Example
- Ordinary: "Who makes the decisions here?"
- Comparison: "Describe for me what qualities in a vendor are important to you, and how that compares with what others [boss, cohorts, department heads, or team members] expect from a vendor." Or, "Tell me how your boss perceives this issue compared to the way you view it."

Competitor Example
- Ordinary: "Who are your competitors?"
- Comparison: "Share with me the qualities that differentiate you from your competitors."

Similar to the benefits of expansion questions, comparison questions garner more information while letting the prospect do the talking. Rather than a question that could give you a stale answer (such as, "Do you have a budget?"), a comparison question will actively engage the prospective customer and ensure that her answer comes with information you can use. A comparison question can also be particularly useful to hone in on important criteria for the prospective customer. When asked whether price is important, an overwhelming majority of people will say yes; however, when asked to rank price, quality, and service, prospective customers will be forced to evaluate their priorities and verbalize what they feel most passionate about.

Let us now return to our sales professional, Mark, and his dealings with National Trucking Corporation. After his first meeting with Lisa, Mark knew that this company would be a complicated sale because of the numerous personalities involved. When Lisa called him back to confirm their appointment with vice president John Williams, Mark was prepared with some more questions about the company and its employees:

Lisa: Well, Mark, I have set up an appointment for you and me to meet with John Williams next Friday at nine. Will that work for you?

Mark: It certainly will, and I thank you again, Lisa, for making that happen. So that we can get the most from this meeting, I want to ask you a few more questions about the company's situation, if you have the time.

Lisa: Sure, that's not a problem at all.

Mark: Great! I want to know if you could explain to me, as the purchasing agent, what is important to you in selecting a vendor, and how does that compare with what is important to John.

Lisa: I am always pressured to keep price low. Every quarter my region is evaluated against other regions throughout the country to see who is operating with the least overhead. Just last month my regional supervisor informed me that my division needs to reduce costs by 15 percent within the next twelve months. That is forcing us to choose the lowest price. As for Williams, when we have been in meetings together, his focus is on increasing revenue.

Mark: Okay, that is always a tricky situation to be in because people feel as if they are being pulled in two different directions. So, what is most important to your company—to cut costs or to increase revenue?

Lisa: Good question. We need to focus on increasing business. Personally, I think everyone has become too anal retentive about cost reductions. Yes, they can be a quick fix, but business is about making a profit. Without a profit the company cannot survive, so that is where our main focus should be.

Mark: Thanks, Lisa. One more question. Could you describe for me what you like about your current system versus what you do not like?

Lisa: Well, the problems I have with our current system have to do with delays. Right now, things can get backed up pretty easily and there is no mechanism to override the system and get everything out on time. These delays cost me money, and I have to stay late in order to make sure that everything is completed. Our current system saves us time when there are no complications, but otherwise it's a hassle.

Mark: Lisa, thanks so much for your time and all of your input. I look forward to our meeting with John Williams on Friday at nine.

Post-Game Analysis: Mark skillfully used comparison questions throughout this second conversation with Lisa to find out information about the company, the current system, and the personalities he would be dealing with in this sale. He can now go into the Friday meeting confident that he has a leg up on the competition because of his knowledge of the prospective customer's business, as well as the issues most pressing in the minds of Lisa and John. Lisa's willingness to share such vital information with Mark also demonstrates her desire to be an advocate and ensure that this sale will go through.

*   *   *

It is Friday morning, and Mark sits down in a boardroom with Lisa, his sales contact, and John Williams, vice president of National Trucking Corporation. After the requisite pleasantries, the three get down to business:

Mark: John, I just want to thank you again for giving me the opportunity to meet with you and Lisa.

John: Well, you come highly recommended by Lisa, so I am ready to hear what you have to say.

Mark: We have done a lot of work in your industry and have great results that I would like to share with you. So that I can zero in on what is most important to you, however, I would like to ask you a few questions first.

John: Fire away!

Mark: It would be very helpful if you could share with me your long-term goals and how they compare with where you are now and where you were twelve months ago. (*Comparison question*)

John: My long-term goal is for this company to become the premier trucking company on the East Coast. In order to do that, we need to ensure that once a customer does business with our company, he will want to come back time and time again. Lately our market share has been suffering because some of our competitors have been slashing their prices in order to drum up business. We are not interested in being the cheapest; however, we are interested in being the best. Twelve months ago we were relatively unknown throughout much of the Southeast, but now, thanks to an aggressive marketing campaign, we have increased our market share by 23 percent in that region. Now we are looking to maintain the quality we have always given our customers, but on a larger scale than ever before.

Mark: Can you walk me through the steps you are taking to make sure that your quality standards are being met? (*Expansion question*)

John: Unfortunately, we have done a poor job at taking steps to reach that goal and my concern is that we will pay the price for not planning ahead. But Lisa assures me that you will be able to help us in that area.

Mark: Well, that's right. Lisa and I talked about the problems she has been having with delays. . . .

Post-Game Analysis: Mark was able to adapt both expansion and comparison questions for his use in this situation. He got the customer talking and placed himself as a solution provider—someone who could help the company achieve its short- and long-term goals. All of the preparation and meetings with Lisa seem to have paid off for him.

* * *

By now you may be thinking that the key to successful sales is simply to go directly to the top; after all, the man or woman at the top is going to be the one making the final decision, right? Not necessarily. Every company is different and each person within a company holds a different portion of power. In the example of the trucking company, the vice president may have been the person to give the final go-ahead for a new contract, but the purchasing agent decides who gets the opportunity to pitch new ideas. Everyone has his or her role to play and your job is to understand those roles. Once you do, you can leverage the relationships and your inside information to create new business opportunities.

This is when you should remember the different influences on your prospective customers' decisions and that those influences certainly translate into both fears and motivations. While the purchasing agent felt the most pressure from her regional supervisor, the vice president was dealing with considerations about his career, as well as how his company fares against the competition. The purchasing agent's goals were more shortsighted than the vice president's because she was evaluated every quarter; the only measure being used was her ability to keep costs low. On the other hand, the vice president was viewed by the company's board of directors as a visionary—someone who would bring the company into the future. Obviously, this would not happen overnight, so he felt more flexibility when making decisions that might not show results immediately.

Understanding these differences is vital if you want to effectively communicate and ultimately do business with both of these people. Expansion questions and comparison questions allow you to probe these relationships and personalities better than ordinary sales questions would. Mark, our salesperson in the trucking example, would never have been privy to so much inside information had he not used comparison and expansion questions to engage the prospective customer and encourage her and her supervisor to do most of the talking.

Exercise 2

1. Write a comparison question that will help you uncover one of the influences affecting your prospective customer.
2. Write a comparison question that asks how the prospective customer's company does its business.
3. Write a comparison question that addresses one of the following topics: competitors, current vendors, or current product usage.

*   *   *

You have learned the importance of asking good questions and engaging customers in the sales process. In this chapter, you were given two relatively simple tools to get the customer to open up and share information with you. The following chapters will provide more tools and slightly more sophisticated questioning techniques. Remember, once you learn the basics of formulating these questions, you can adapt them to fit any sales situation.

Are You a Consultant or a Product Peddler? The Educational Question

IN MY EXPERIENCE, most salespeople do not wish to be seen simply as "product peddlers." Most salespeople sincerely want to help their prospective customers by improving their business, saving them money, and expanding their share of the market. The problem is that many prospects are cynical. They either were burned by an unscrupulous salesperson in the past or know someone who was. This makes them leery of new salespeople.

To get over this hurdle, salespeople need to position themselves as experts or advisers who use their expertise to improve the lives of their prospective customers. Using the educational questions will help you build trust and rapport quickly with prospective clients.

Educational questions are expanded forms of comparison questions. They give prospects the opportunity to voice their opinions and allow you to see how they feel about various business issues. Often the best way to connect with your prospective customers is to present yourself as an informational resource, rather than someone who is "checking in."

Using the example of a pharmaceutical sales rep, let's see how asking educational questions helps him establish a sales relationship with a respected pediatrician:

Rep: Doctor, I was reading an article in *Time* magazine last week that discussed the growing problems pediatricians face when counseling patients and patients' families about obesity. The article claimed that many families are in denial about their children's weight issues and poor eating habits, and they tend to shrug off warnings from their pediatrician about how unhealthy lifestyles lead to problems later on. Could you share with me how your experience compares with what the article claims?

Dr.: We encounter that problem every week. Some families are totally out of touch when it comes to healthful eating. I just met with a mother and father of three boys who were so proud because they had cut down their fast-food intake from five times a week to only four! Unfortunately, there are parents out there who are clueless about how their food choices affect their children.

Educational questions allow you, as a salesperson, to take on the role of consultant—someone who knows what is going on in the marketplace and in the research centers. When asking an educational question, you not only engage the prospective customer in talk about controversial issues but also present yourself as someone with fresh information, rather than simply trying to sell your product. The educational question is easy to compose because it requires only that you keep up with the latest news in your industry, as well as other trends or issues affecting a prospect's business—something you probably do already.

The goal in using the educational question is to engage your prospective customers by sharing information that is relevant to their problems. The key is to make the prospective client feel understood, and most of all understood by you. These questions are not meant to be used manipulatively; rather, they are intended to stimulate a prospect's thinking and encourage exploration of options. Once you have started a prospect thinking about different possibilities and new ways of doing business, your product will almost inevitably be seen as a solution.

A Template for Educational Questions

"I read recently in an article in _____ [any reputable news source or industry journal—for example, *New York Times, Wall Street Journal, U.S. News & World Report, Journal of the American Medical Association, Business Week,* or *The Economist*] that _____

_____

[give a brief summary of the article's main points]. Tell me, how does that compare with what you are seeing?"

For example:

- "Last week I read an article in the *Wall Street Journal* that claimed drug testing is an ineffective tool to weed out poor-quality job applicants. Yet, five times as many companies test for drugs today compared to ten years ago. What has been your experience on this issue?"
- "A recent article in *U.S. News & World Report* stated that over 75 percent of high-tech firms today turn to foreign workers to manage their help-desk operations. One of the key challenges seems to be the language barrier and the difficulty customers have had communicating with the new help desk. How do you feel about this growing trend?"
- "In the newest issue of the *Journal of the American Medical Association* the editors applauded new laws that prohibit doctors from accepting gifts or favors from pharmaceutical companies. Some doctors, however, are claiming these laws are discriminatory. How do you feel about these recent changes?"
- "This morning's *New York Times* quoted the Federal Reserve chairman as saying he wanted to raise interest rates at least one percentage point before the end of the year. Many small businesses are concerned that this will significantly impact their ability to hold down costs. What are your thoughts and how might this affect your business?"

These examples help to illustrate the various ways in which educational questions can be used. You should have a plan in place to transition the meeting from the educational question to the concerns of the individual with whom you are meeting. They will not always lead directly into a discussion of your product or service, but a good educational question should lay the groundwork for an exchange of ideas and provoke a response from your prospective customer.

Once you have asked an educational question, you will need to listen carefully to the response and tailor your follow-up questions accordingly. This will help ensure that the conversation heads in the direction where you can offer help to the prospective customer.

The information you use for an educational question does not necessarily need to come from a printed source. As a salesperson, you interact with numerous people in your industry every day. By prefacing your question with the statement, "Some of my other clients have been telling me," you'll find that your prospective customer will more fully appreciate your ability to share vital information. An educational question, strategically placed in a meeting, will enable you to probe the prospective customer's feelings and stimulate conversation.

Timing the Educational Question

There are three key times when an educational question will be most useful. First, educational questions can be used as a teaser on a voice mail message; second, as an icebreaker at the beginning of a meeting; and, third, as a way to stimulate conversation during a lull in a meeting.

The first instance is probably the simplest to execute. We have all experienced days almost entirely spent on the phone, leaving voicemail messages for prospective and current customers only to see none of those calls returned. Rather than simply leaving your name and number (or worse, a three-minute speech about your product), leave an educational question that conveys a sense of importance, even urgency. For example, consider a voice mail message left by a member of a marketing firm for an insurance executive:

> Hi, Bill; this is Jenna. I happened to be reading an article this morning in the *Wall Street Journal* that I thought would be of interest to you. The article quoted an industry insider saying that increased state and federal regulations will force a number of agencies in the Southeast to either consolidate or close their doors. However, a number of firms I've spoken to want to capitalize on these changes by terminating unprofitable business and focusing their efforts on more lucrative markets. Anyway, I was just wondering if you had seen the article and what you thought about it. Why don't you give me a call and I can share some ideas on what other firms are doing. Thanks!

Although Bill was most likely already aware of the changes in state and federal regulations, Jenna brought those changes to the surface and presented herself as someone who could help provide some answers in his quest for more business.

As mentioned, an educational question can also be an icebreaker, a way to begin a conversation and build rapport with a prospective customer.

Using the question this way not only will inspire your prospective customer to start talking but also alleviate some of the pressure of "the sale." Unlike other questions, the educational question does not immediately steer the prospective customer toward buying your product or service. Instead of pushing the sale, you use the educational question to allow the prospective customer to voice her feelings, to vent and to relate to you as a consultant. But let us look at an example of the educational question used as an ice-breaker.

Lucas needs to find a new way to break the ice during his next meeting. He had asked his last prospective customer about his hobbies and then, unfortunately, was forced to sit through a twenty-minute diatribe about how hard it is to get tee time in the city. Eventually, the prospect looked at his watch and mumbled something about having to go to another meeting. Lucas realized that he could not risk that happening again.

As he sits down to read *Investors Business Daily*, he notices an article about employers tracking their employees' use of the Internet. Lucas works as a consultant specializing in employee productivity, and now he has his hook. He refers to the article during his next meeting with Larry, the IT director of a large banking conglomerate:

Lucas: Just this morning, I read an article in the *Investors Business Daily* that said that employees in large companies spend more than an hour each day on the Internet for personal reasons. The article went on to say that it costs a typical Fortune 1000 company millions of dollars annually. I'm curious as to what your thoughts are about this issue.

Larry: It's interesting that you bring this up, as we talked about the problem at last month's board meeting. But we are not sure exactly what the legalities are surrounding the issue, and we wonder how the employees would feel if we kept tabs on them. Did the article mention those issues at all?

Post-Game Analysis: Although this particular question might not lead to any business for Lucas, he will certainly stick out in the IT director's mind as a rich source of information—someone who is credible and should be looked to when a need arises.

* * *

The third way educational questions can be used is during a lull in the conversation, or when you cannot seem to engage a prospective customer even after using expansion and comparison questions. Prospects attempting to stay noncommittal during a sales meeting will be forced to give their opinion when asked an educational question. This will allow you to find out how they really feel about the subject and will help you avoid filling the time with idle chatter about the weather. Educational questions force prospects to take a side; they cannot "sit on the fence" when asked their opinion.

The educational question demands that the prospective customer take a stand, and when he does, his emotions automatically show through. Here is another example of an educational question, this time used to get the individual to take a position.

Kathy, who works for an employee benefits company, has been struggling through a frustrating meeting for the last thirty minutes. She has tried to get Marla, the president of a construction company, to communicate her frustrations and motivations, but Marla sits there like a stone wall. Kathy decides that none of her expansion or comparison questions will provoke a response from Marla, so Kathy tries to at least get Marla to express an opinion about something:

Kathy: As you know, attracting high-quality applicants is an ongoing struggle for many construction firms. *Kiplinger Reports* states that quality health-care coverage is what employees want most. Others disagree, saying that what people want most is competitive hourly pay. What are your thoughts on what seem to be two opposing viewpoints?

Marla: Actually, we've been struggling with this issue for some time. The rates for coverage have been increasing about 15 percent annually for the last five years. We already have a lot of pressure to attract and maintain a quality workforce. Granted, an eighteen-year-old may not care about insurance coverage because he thinks he is superman. But the average age of our workforce is twenty-seven and most of our guys have families. Therefore, health-care coverage is a necessity. In fact, we've tried cheaper plans and they did not work. We have found this subject coming up in our exit interviews when employees leave our company. We discovered that talented people were leaving because our competitors offered better plans.

Kathy: Well, my company has a proven track record in your industry. Our experience means that we can come up with some very creative yet competitive health-care plans that will not only attract good-quality applicants but reduce employee turnover.

Marla: Yes, we should talk about that. I am certainly familiar with your firm's reputation. In fact, do you have some time available to meet with my human resources director, who is responsible for managing benefits?

Post-Game Analysis: Obviously, every educational question will not lead to a new contract with a prospective customer. These questions do provide the opportunity, however, for you to make inroads and establish yourself as a partner rather than simply someone trying to sell a product. An educational question also provides a good alternative to the customary questions thrown at established customers. Instead of asking, "Is there anything I can do for you today?" or "How are things going?" you can bring some information to the table. By bringing fresh ideas and a new perspective to your clients, you will not only help them but also be cementing in the position for yourself as consultant.

* * *

By now you may be asking yourself: Why do I need to be seen as a partner? How will that help me in the long run, after I have gotten the contract? Those are very good questions, with very important answers. One answer is that a salesperson who is not seen as a partner will often become expendable if a new, cheaper product comes into town. If all you are providing to your customers is a product or service, then the deciding factor when your customer is weighing a change in vendor becomes the price. Even though you might have built a relationship and had good rapport with your customer, another salesperson can offer the same product at a 10 percent discount and can easily take your place.

Exercise 1

By now, you know the drill when it comes to these exercises. Create three educational questions that you could use during meetings with prospective customers.

1. Formulate an educational question that can serve as an icebreaker at a meeting with someone in your industry.
2. Formulate an educational question that you can use to find out someone's opinion about a hot topic in your industry.

3. Formulate an educational question that can invigorate a dying conversation. It does not have to be related to your product or service—simply write a question that will get your prospective customer involved in the conversation.

Some Final Examples of Educational Questions

- "The intense changes in technology have been especially influential on your industry. According to *U.S. News & World Report,* many hospitals are experiencing greater _____. What are you experiencing?"
- "In reading about your industry in the latest *Fortune* magazine, I have picked up on three major changes/trends/issues. They are _____. Which one do you see as most important?"
- "Could you share with me how your experience compares with what the article claims about _____?"
- "How does the new legislation regarding _____ change the way you do business?"
- "Do you expect this trend as reported in the *New York Times* to encourage or inhibit growth?"

Educational questions are great because they take advantage of something you are doing already—keeping up with industry news and trends—while elevating your status in the eyes of prospective and current customers. Do not try to pepper every conversation with educational questions, however, because it will not appear natural. One educational question per meeting is enough to solidify your role as consultant.

Directing the Conversation: Lock-On and Impact Questions

SO FAR, I have given you several types of questions to use as tools when meeting with prospective and current customers. By now you may be wondering, what do I do with all of the information I get from my customers after I ask these questions? How do I manage the conversation while still allowing the customer to vent and discuss problems? If I let the customer do all the talking, how will we ever get anywhere in the conversation? The answer to these questions lies in the next tool I will introduce you to, the lock-on question.

A lock-on question maintains the flow of a natural conversation while providing a way to steer the discussion in certain directions. By using a lock-on question, you can zero in on a particular point of interest and direct the customer's attention to that point. This saves you time and energy and ultimately provides the customer with a solution in a short amount of time.

Another benefit of the lock-on question is its ability to clarify the thoughts and feelings of your customers. Oftentimes in conversation customers will use words and phrases such as *quality, partnership,* or *streamlining the process* without really defining them. Lock-on questions enable you to get into a customer's head to determine what is really meant. The business world is dominated by jargon. Words are often used with little or no meaning attached to them; sometimes even the customer does not know exactly what his words mean. Through your use of lock-on questions, you have the incredible opportunity to hear customers articulate their problems and expand on their ideas.

Dartnell Research, a leading research firm, has found that customers do not verbalize their real concerns and problems 80 percent of the time; rather, customers tend to conceal issues that might reveal vulnerability. If you use lock-on questions, though, you can force customers to open up. Instead of becoming bogged down in jargon and superficiality, the conversation is immersed in facts and experiences that really matter. You can then use the information to tap into the customer's emotions, beliefs, and values through impact and vision questions. In this chapter, you will learn how to use lock-on questions, when to use them, and why they allow you to manage conversations. Then, you will be introduced to the power of impact questions: questions that encourage customers to calculate the costs of *not* doing business with you. In the following chapter, you will discover the power of vision questions to cement the partnership you have been building with your customers.

How to Create Lock-On Questions

Now that you know what lock-on questions do for you, here are some examples of them in action:

Customer: We have been trying to get this project off the ground for several months.

Lock-on question: I noticed you said the word *trying*. What has worked so far and what has not?

Trying is the key word to focus on in this example. The word represents feelings of frustration and discouragement at not being able to achieve a goal. Here, the customer has given you a great opportunity to bring the problems to the surface, to have her relive those feelings and then look to you for a solution.

Customer: I am looking for a partnership rather than just someone to sell me a product.

Lock-on question: Could you give me some specifics of what you mean when you say *partnership*?

Partnership is just one example of business jargon, with little real meaning. Although as a salesperson you might see *partnership* as a way to provide real value to the customer while improving your business, many customers use the term to force vendors into price concessions. For example, the Big Three automakers frequently use the word with their suppliers as a way to induce lower costs. For you as a salesperson, then, it is important to define the customer's term.

Customer: My company has been experiencing problems with our current vendor and we are looking for someone new.

Lock-on question: Can you give me an example of the problems you have been experiencing? [*What better way for your customer to relive a painful situation created by a vendor?*]

The power that comes from asking for examples cannot be overemphasized. A customer who reveals a past problem experiences again the emotional trauma of that problem. He not only confides in you but also provides details of his business and his criteria for a vendor.

Customer: Our goal for this quarter is to reduce costs by 10 percent, but we have found this to be very challenging.

Lock-on question: When you say it has been challenging, what exactly do you mean?

Similar to the example of *trying*, the word *challenging* connotes negative emotions and aggravation owing to unattained goals. A lock-on question will help the customer vent those emotions and supply specifics that you can use to promote your product.

As you can see in these examples, lock-on questions work by providing answers that help you hone in on a certain aspect of a customer's statement. You can then either clarify the words she is using or direct the conversation according to your needs. Here are some words and phrases that can be easily used to create lock-on questions:

Trying to

Dealing with

Problems

Concerns

Hopeful

Unclear

Stressful

Seeking

Needs

Improvement

Struggling

Having difficulties

Challenges

Afraid

Frustrated

Doubts

Searching

Looking for

Goals

These words and others like them signal that a customer's needs are not being completely met. They allow you to focus on the areas of concern and to uncover ways to address those concerns. The words are almost all revealing of emotions and indicate a realization that there is a problem to be solved.

After identifying these words and using lock-on questions to discover the problems, you can present yourself as the solution provider. Your customer will be grateful that you have isolated the problem and helped to create the solution. As was the case with the educational question, after you've used a lock-on question, you will be seen as a valuable partner in business, rather than someone who simply sells a product or provides a service.

There are other indicators customers use that can be "locked on" and turned into great questions. One example is the use of the terms *we* or *us*. It may seem obvious, but any time a customer uses the editorial *we* or other plural pronouns, you know that there is more than one decision maker and more than one person who recognizes the problem. These are great words to lock-on to by asking, "I noticed you mentioned the word *we*; who else is involved in this problem?" The key to using lock-on questions successfully is to listen closely to what your customers say and then ask them questions filled with their own words.

Remember, when your customers give you these key words, they have opened the door for you to enter their minds. You should not feel like you are prying or being nosy. Customers want to talk about problems, frustrations, and concerns but often they do not know how to bring them up in conversation.

When to Use Lock-On Questions

Just like the other question types introduced in this book, lock-on questions arc not designed to be used continuously in a meeting. A conversation generously peppered with lock-on questions would seem false and uncomfortable for a customer and would not allow you to follow the logical progression of the meeting. Owing to their personal nature, lock-on questions should also not be used at the very beginning of a relationship. A customer faced with lock-on questions after just meeting you might think you are being insincere or even sarcastic. Lock-on questions used too frequently can also make a customer feel as if he is being interrogated. You must make sure that you understand these conditions and rules before you engage in lock-on questioning. Use lock-on questions when:

- You have a good rapport with the customer and have demonstrated empathy toward him.
- You have a sincere desire to connect with the customer.
- You respect the level of information your customer feels comfortable sharing.
- You avoid problems to which you cannot offer a solution.
- You focus on problems your competition is not addressing.
- You avoid problems that you or your company may have created in the past for this customer.

Once you understand and accept these rules for using lock-on questions, you are ready to try this technique with customers. Also, if you feel lock-on questions will be viewed as too direct, you can use buffer statements to preface your question. Some examples of buffer statements include:

"Help me understand. . . ."

"When you say the word. . . ."

"Could you clarify for me. . . ."

"What is an example that comes to mind. . . ."

Exercise 1

After each customer statement, lock on to some of the words or phrases in that statement and use them to create possible lock-on questions. In the first example I have given you a little help by putting in italics some of the words you could use to form your question. Write as many lock-on questions you can think of.

1. "*We* have been *looking* at a few *options* to *better meet* our *needs.*" How many lock-on questions were you able to formulate from that simple statement? Let's hope you managed to come up with at least five or six questions for this opportunity. See "Some Examples of Lock-On Questions" for possible questions.
2. "Most of us agree that we should improve quality and performance while reducing overhead, all the while finding a vendor who can listen to our needs."
3. "My department has been reprimanded for not meeting our profit goals."
4. "At this time we are struggling with a newly competitive market driven almost entirely by price."

Some Examples of Lock-On Questions

Here are some possible responses to the first item in Exercise 1:

- "You mentioned you were looking; for how long have you been looking?"
- "What prompted you to start looking?"
- "What options have you considered?"
- "What options have you eliminated?"
- "You mentioned *have been*; does that mean you are still looking?"
- "What needs are not currently being met?"

- "For how long have your needs not been met?"
- "What criteria are you using to determine who can best meet your needs?"
- "Which of your needs are most important and which are least important?"
- "You mentioned *we*; who else has input into this decision?"
- "How will the decision to pursue a new option be made?"
- "Let's assume your needs can be met; what do you hope to accomplish?"

By now you should be able to appreciate all of the opportunities secured when you use lock-on questions. It is important to remember, however, that lock-on questions cannot be effective if you do not listen to your customers. Too many of us have fallen into the habit of not listening to the answers our customers give. I know I have made this mistake myself. Instead of listening, I am thinking of my next question! Lock-on questions not only force you to listen; they also take the pressure off of you to think of another question. The question will appear right in front of you—if only you listen to your customer's words.

The lock-on questioning technique is difficult for many salespeople to embrace. So many sales professionals are programmed with their own agendas, they want to provide a solution without really listening to the problem. It is unfortunate that so many of us have become arrogant in our belief that we know what is best for our customers. The truth is that every situation is different. Even if you are thinking, "I've heard this a dozen times before," in reality the customer has specific concerns and individual motivations that you cannot possibly know unless she tells you. Lock-on questions not only provide a tool to use in your meetings; they also force you to take the time to listen to your customers.

How to Manage a Conversation Using Lock-On Questions

Now that you have learned how to focus on a customer's emotions using the lock-on technique, you can begin to appreciate other ways it can be used. Many salespeople are wary at first about my system of questioning because they are afraid of losing control of the conversation. What they do not realize is that by asking the questions, they are the ones in control.

Asking the customer questions gives you the power to direct the conversation, instead of simply presenting your product and hoping the customer becomes interested.

For example, Katherine sells clothing to department and discount stores, but she has been on the job only for a few months and has yet to have real success. She has spent the last week calling different stores to discuss her company's clothing line and still does not have a client to call her own. This morning, she is able to land a call with the vice president of purchasing for a major discount store. Katherine hopes that this potential sale will be the one to finally put her on the map. Here's what happens:

The vice president confides in Katherine that the store's executives had recently held a meeting to discuss problems with their current vendor. This is the perfect moment for Katherine to use a lock-on question to uncover the exact nature of those problems. Katherine asks, "You mentioned your current vendor was not meeting your expectations; could you give me an example of exactly what happened?" Once the vice president starts talking, Katherine can easily find other questions to ask regarding the store's situation. She can then use this information to tailor her presentation to meet the specific needs of that store.

But Katherine needs to determine the level of commitment to change at which the store executives are operating. As all of us in business know, there are hundreds of meetings a year about changes that should be made but never are. Instead of assuming that a company has committed to making a change, Katherine has to examine its words and actions to determine where it is in the decision-making process. One of the initial ways to do this is to "qualify" the opportunity, using the techniques spelled out in Chapter 3. After qualifying, though, Katherine still needs to discover the stage of commitment in order to understand whether the company is ready to make a change in vendor, product, or service.

The Stages of Commitment

There are three stages of commitment: Should, Want To, and Have To. In the Should phase, the customer does not have the desire to change and does not see the need for change. In the Want To phase, the customer wants to change and recognizes the need to change but resists taking action. In the Have To phase, the customer stands ready to make a change and will embrace a solution tailored to the company's needs.

By simply listening to the words the vice president uses, Katherine can learn the level of readiness of the store's executives and then use that knowledge to bring them into the Have To phase. Figure 6-1 on the next page lists examples of words and behaviors of customers and their corresponding stages of commitment.

Katherine also needs to encourage the vice-president to relive the problems caused by the current vendor and explain what those problems meant for the company. A simple way to do this is for Katherine to ask the vice president, "What have been some of the immediate effects of the problems with your current vendor?" Once Katherine brings these problems and their negative effects to the surface, she can then easily present herself as a sensible alternative to the current vendor. Let's look at how Katherine can take advantage of the situation by using a lock-on question:

Vice President: Well, this is a pretty big coincidence. We just had a meeting two days ago to discuss how our current vendors were not exactly meeting our expectations. Would you be willing to come out for a presentation?

Katherine: I would be delighted to put together a presentation for your company, but before I do that I'd like to know a little more about your situation. Could you give me an example of a time when your current vendor did not meet your expectations? (Lock-on question)

Vice President: Something happened just last month, as a matter of fact. We were supposed to get shipments of 10,000 bathing suits to our stores nationwide. Our supplier, Shag Clothing, failed to get us the shipments on time—in fact, the swimsuits did not get to our stores for four weeks! Obviously, we expect our vendors to deliver the promised goods on time, but unfortunately our expectations were not met in this situation.

Katherine capitalized on a few comments made by the customer. She used a lock-on question and benefited in two ways: She found out more about the customer's business, and she succeeded in having the customer verbalize a problem with the current vendor.

Once you have gotten a customer to this point, it is time to move beyond the lock-on questions and enter a new phase: the impact question. In this phase, you will be using the information you learned so far in the meeting to get the customer to recognize how problematic the situation really is with the current vendor.

FIGURE 6-1. Customer behaviors in three stages of commitment.

	Should	**Want to**	**Have to**
Customer behavior	The customer responds to your questions with vague answers. The customer does not recognize that she has a problem. Rather than answering your questions, she lets you talk.	The customer willingly shares problems and frustrations. Although the customer recognizes that there is a problem, she is not yet ready to take action to remedy the problem.	The customer knows that the benefits of change outweigh the risks of staying in the current situation. The customer is eager to talk about solutions. Only about 10 percent of customers will be in the **Have to** phase on their own; others will need your guidance to get there.
Words and phrases to look for	Maybe We'll see Not right now I'm too busy	Considering Thinking about We would like to We need to We are looking at We want to	Must Will Definitely Have to Can't afford not to We are ready
What you can do at this stage	Determine why the client lacks desire; maybe the problem is not affecting him directly. You could look for other contacts at the company or decide that the company itself is not yet ready to make a decision. Remember, there is not always an opportunity to be had.	**Do not** try to sell your product/ service at this stage because you will only meet resistance. Instead, uncover the motivations to change and then use those to get the customer to the **Have to** phase. One way to do this is to help him see that the benefits (ROI) outweigh the costs of his current situation.	If you encounter a customer in this phase you are lucky. All you will need to do is guide him through the problems he is facing and how your solution can solve those problems. Remember, most customers will not be at the **Have to** phase when you first meet with them.

How to Use Impact Questions

It is not enough to bring your customer's problems to the surface; you also need to help your customer quantify these problems. A customer who does not appreciate the size of the problem will not be motivated to change. The way to achieve this motivation is through the use of the impact question. Impact questions take customers through the problem, asking them to relive it and calculate how it affects the company and themselves.

The impact question often begins with coaching a customer into calculating how much money is lost by staying with the current vendor, product, or service. Let's look at an example of this approach that Katherine can use with the vice president and then we will discuss the second part of impact questions:

Vice President: Something happened just last month, as a matter of fact. We were supposed to get shipments of 10,000 bathing suits to our stores nationwide. Our supplier, Shag Clothing, failed to get us the shipments on time—in fact, the swimsuits did not get to our stores for four weeks! Obviously, we expect our vendors to deliver the promised goods on time, but unfortunately our expectations were not met in this situation.

Katherine: What effects did this delay have on your company?

Vice President: This delay definitely had some negative effects on the company. The shopping season for swimsuits is surprisingly short, so missing out on four weeks is equivalent to missing half of the season. Plus, we had empty swimsuit racks right in the front of our stores!

Katherine: How much do you charge for these swimsuits?

Vice President: We usually charge about $30 per suit. This year we missed half of the season. We expected to sell 10,000 swimsuits but we sold only about 2,500.

Katherine: This means that 7,500 swimsuits were left in inventory and you lost approximately $225,000 in revenue. Does that seem correct?

Vice President: Yes.

Katherine: While we're at it, let me ask you something else. How much does your average customer spend when she comes into your store?

Vice President: We have found that our average customer spends $200 each time she visits our store. Owing to our wide variety of merchandise, everything from sneakers to soap, we generally have customers come in looking for one thing but ending up buying multiple items.

Katherine: Do you think it's possible that when some of your customers came in looking for swimsuits and saw the empty racks they turned around and left without buying anything else?

Vice President: Sure, according to Gartner Group, whom we rely on for retail shopping trends, 20 percent of customers will leave if the particular product they came for is not on the shelf.

Katherine: What is your estimate of how many customers may have walked out during that four-week period when the suits were not on the racks?

Vice President: I would not be surprised if the number is somewhere around 2,000 people.

Katherine: So 2,000 times $200 per person equals $400,000 of lost revenue. Would that be about right?

Vice President: Yes, I believe that's about right.

Katherine: Just this one incident cost you $625,000! How many times do you experience something like this in a given year?

Vice President: Unfortunately, with this vendor we experience a problem like this about once a quarter.

Katherine: What would that equate to in terms of lost revenue?

Vice President: [Long sigh] My guess would be about $1.8 million.

Katherine: $1.8 million per year. What does that translate to in terms of your overall revenue for the year?

Vice President: That's almost 2 percent of our revenue for the year. It's crazy to lose that because of a vendor.

As you can see, coaching your customer to quantify the problem is not simple. It requires a little patience on your part, but the effects are priceless. In the above example, Katherine got her customer to realize that the company was losing $1.8 million per year because of a vendor. How could the company *not* make a change after that realization? Most customers do not recognize the extent of their problems, and it is your job, through questioning, to transform those problems into dollar signs.

After the customer has quantified the problem and put a dollar value on it, you can move to the second step of the impact question. At this point, you question the customer about the impact of the problem (in this case it's a problem with the vendor) on the company, the customer's position in the company, and the customer's personal well-being. You need to drive home all of the negative effects of the current situation until your customer almost hits rock bottom.

Impact questions get the customer to take a step back and view the entire picture. Rather than remaining wrapped up in the day-to-day issues, the customer meets the challenge of looking into the future and seeing what could happen if the current problem does not get resolved. Here's an example of Katherine using the impact questions:

Katherine: $1.8 million per year. What does that translate to in terms of your overall revenue for the year?

Vice President: That's almost 2 percent of our revenue for the year. It's crazy to lose that because of a vendor.

Katherine: What about the time you and other personnel have to spend tracking down late deliveries? Or the overtime needed to stock shelves at the last minute?

Vice President: It's funny you should ask. Last Saturday I had to spend twelve hours here working to fill empty shelves because of this problem. I had to cancel plans to watch my kid's Little League game. I was really upset and so was my son.

Katherine: That must have been frustrating. I know I hate it when I have to leave my kids in order to do something at work. If I could summarize this issue, what you have shared with me is a problem that is costing your company $1.8 million a year and it's costing you personally with time you could be spending with your family. What do you think the impact on your company will be if you decide to do nothing and stay with your current vendor? [Here's the first impact question, targeting the effects on the company.]

Vice President: To tell you the truth, I can't believe that we have put up with this problem for so long. A loss of $1.8 million is a huge financial drain on our company. This conversation has made me realize that we cannot afford *not* to change vendors. [Now the customer is in the Have To phase and is ready to make a change.]

Katherine: What impact do you think this problem could have on you within your company? [The second impact question, targeting the effects on the customer's role in the company]

Vice President: If we continue to lose money like this, I can't imagine I would be able to keep my job for much longer. I don't know what I would do if that happened. [She has helped the customer recognize the problem and take ownership of it. Instead of telling him, she helped him realize how devastating this situation was for his company and himself.]

Katherine: I understand. At one time or another, I think we have all feared for our jobs. You also mentioned losing time with your kids. Do you think that situation will change if your problem continues? [The third impact question, targeting the effects on the customer's personal life]

Vice President: Unless we switch vendors, I foresee more late nights and weekends spent here instead of with my kids, and I do not want that to happen. We need to do something right now about this situation! [She has discovered what the customer values; in this case, it is time with his family. Now she will be able to situate her product as a solution to his problem, and consequently a way for him to spend more time doing the things he wants to do and less time dealing with problems at work.]

Katherine: Okay, why don't we talk about the presentation?

As you can see, impact questions really emphasize the seriousness of the customer's problem. You must use your own discretion when determining how far to go with a customer. When I teach this skill to salespeople, they are often concerned about using impact questions. Many seem to believe that the questions are too personal or too controversial. In the example above, though, it is the vice president (not the salesperson) who brought up the topic of family, as well as the possibility of losing his job. Once the customer opens that proverbial door, he has invited you to discuss those topics.

Rather than shy away from tough subjects, you as the salesperson should embrace them to discover how to best help your customer. It is important to remember that as long as you are sincere in your exchange with a customer, you will both benefit. If you were to use impact questions only to scare a customer into doing business with you, that would be manipulation.

How Impact Questions Encourage Change

Most people are reluctant to change unless their situation demands it. Even when people face a problem, they usually try to just deal with it instead of looking for a way to solve it. It is easier to avoid the proverbial pothole than to fill it. So, as a salesperson, your job is to use questions to highlight a customer's problem and help your customer discover for himself the magnitude of the problem.

Too many salespeople jump on their customer with a solution as soon as the customer mentions a problem. If you do this, you will deny the customer her time to vent. Let your customer have as much time as she wants to lament her situation. Ask questions about how the problem is impacting her job, her department, her company, and her customers. Once she has expressed all of these frustrations, she will be eager to buy from you

In most cases, customers have never taken the time to analyze their problems, nor do they calculate exactly how much a particular issue costs them. If you can take your customers through that process, so that they can figure out for themselves how much money, time, resources, and aggravation are involved in avoiding their problems, they will see how important it is to fix them.

Sample Impact Questions

- "How does this problem affect sales? Profitability? Scheduling? On-time deliveries? Quality? Production?"
- "What do you think these problems are costing you?"
- "How is this problem impacting the bottom line?"
- "How much time do you spend each day dealing with this problem? If you could free up this time, what other tasks would you prefer doing?"
- "How many employees have to address this problem? How much does it cost to train and employ these people?"
- "When you have these difficulties with quality, how much does it cost you to fix them?"
- "Have you lost customers because of this problem? How much were those customers worth to you?"
- "How is this problem affecting other areas of your business?"

- "Let's assume you decide not to address this problem right away. What will that cost you this year?"
- "If you do not fix this problem, what is the potential impact on your business? Can you afford to take that risk?"
- "Can your company achieve its stated goals without addressing this problem?"
- "Are you able to devote sufficient time to other projects while dealing with this problem?"
- "Has company morale been affected by this problem? Have people left over this issue?"
- "How much does it cost to recruit and train a new employee? How long does it take before a new person can perform his job without supervision? How much does that lost time cost you?"

Once you have taken your customer through the series of impact questions and he has recognized the need for change, present him with a brighter picture of the future. This is when vision questions come into play. This question type not only lifts the customer's spirits but also positions you as the person who can present the solution. Vision questions are explained in the next chapter.

Back to the Future: Vision Questions

AFTER TAKING A CUSTOMER through a series of impact questions, you will have someone in front of you who will want desperately to make a change. Vision questions enable you to show the customer a bright future, to present him with a picture of what could be if he did business with you. Whereas impact questions were all about emphasizing the negative effects of a customer's current situation, vision questions focus on the positive results that can be achieved.

At first, abstract questions concerning your customer's future might seem strange to you. Most salespeople are much more comfortable asking questions about the present than about the past or future. The positive effects of vision questions, however, cannot be denied. When your customer can envision a future without her current problems, a future that might even include a raise or a chance to work fewer hours, she will be your most ardent supporter. Just like impact questions, vision questions often work best in a series, beginning with the effects a change in vendor or service provider will have on the company and then progressively on the person with whom you are dealing.

Vision questions usually have the word *if* in them. These questions are very powerful because they tap into your customer's needs and desires for the future. Vision questions get people to articulate their emotions; this is what motivates people to take action. Your customer has hopes and dreams just like you do. Your job is to help him reach those dreams. You do this by getting your customer to articulate her goals and then mapping out the path that will take her there. The path, of course, is your product or service. The key is to get your customer to articulate the path, instead of jumping in and pitching the solution yourself. Do not try to be your customer's hero; be a supportive coach instead.

A Series of Generic Vision Questions

- "If we could eliminate that problem you are currently experiencing, that problem that is costing you [for example] $1 million per year, what effects do you think that would have on your company?"
- "If we could implement that change, how do you think that would affect your position and goals within the company?"
- "How would implementing this change affect you personally? What would you be able to do differently?"

In particular, posing a vision question that touches on the person often makes salespeople uneasy. However, we all know that a person's experiences at work affect his time at home. Many people view working long hours and weekends as a necessary evil, rather than a sacrifice they are making for the good of the company. If you are able to offer a solution that will not only help the company but also make your customer's life easier, you will be a hero!

What Your Customer Needs

You might be wondering why your customers have never talked to you about their desire for more time with their families or their wish for a raise. People have been conditioned in our society not to expose too much and to avoid seeming vulnerable. Customers embrace these mores by masking their real wants with superficial needs.

The best way to understand this concept is through the dichotomy of explicit needs and implicit needs. Explicit needs are those needs most commonly expressed by customers when asked what they are looking for. Some examples of explicit needs include improving service or quality, growing the market share, and reducing overhead. These needs tend to be based on measurable factors such as price or percentage, but they do not go to the heart of why customers do what they do. For that, we must look at implicit needs.

Implicit needs are the driving force behind most of what we do each day, and they can be broken down into five categories:

1. **Success.** This is the need to feel a sense of accomplishment when you come home from a long day of work. Even if customers do not get any immediate gratification from completing a deal, that feeling of accomplishment and achievement motivates them to strive toward the goal and see the transaction through. Customers who are looking for this need to be met will often talk about wanting to "get the job done" or "look for a sense of satisfaction."

2. **Independence.** This is the need to feel some measure of *control* at work. Many of our customers have several bosses to report to, as well as shareholders breathing down their necks. When a customer can make a decision on his own, he feels in charge of his own destiny, rather than as a cog in the wheel. Customers who are looking for this need to be met will often mention yearning for "the opportunity to be creative" or "trust from my bosses to make my own decision."

3. **Recognition.** This is the need to feel valued as a worker and to feel that your opinions matter. Even though we are paid for our work, almost all of us still look for that "pat on the back," the signal from our boss that our efforts have been noticed. No one wants to go to work every day and feel that her voice is not heard. One salesperson told me that the worst day of her life was when she was told not to bother coming to a meeting. She realized then that her hard work was not being recognized and that she had become nearly invisible within her own company. Customers who are looking for this need to be met might discuss wanting "everyone to realize all of the hard work I do" or "people to really pay attention when I talk in board meetings."

4. **Security.** This need is twofold: It is the need to feel that your job will not be taken away from you and it's the desire to save face and not look stupid. Although many salespeople recognize the fear their customers have of losing their jobs, most do not take into account the need of their customers to avoid embarrassment and criticism by peers and bosses. When a customer you are dealing with seems reluctant, and even procrastinates making a decision, he just may be apprehensive about making the wrong decision. As salespeople, we cannot give our customers any guarantees about their jobs, but we can give them the tools to show

their superiors how vital they are to the company's operation. Customers who are looking for this need to be met might mention being "afraid that their job could be in jeopardy" or use key words such as *concerned, worried, unsure, afraid, troubled,* or *doubtful.*

5. **Stimulation.** This is the need to feel challenged by your job, to go to work every day and feel exhilarated instead of bored. We all have heard customers lament busy schedules and crazy deadlines, but even worse than those people are the customers who sit at their desks each day uninspired by the jobs in front of them. People enjoy using all of their faculties to solve a problem and often thrive on that situation. Customers who are looking for this need to be met will probably talk about the tasks they dislike or the everyday "fires" to put out.

These implicit needs will motivate your customers to do business with you, but only if you recognize those needs. Once you understand which implicit need your customer wants met, you can use vision questions to address that need. The next exercise will ask you to determine, based on a few sentences from a customer, the implicit need *not* being met.

Exercise 1

Read the following statements from customers and then determine which implicit need he or she wants to be met:

1. "It's tough because I have only worked here for a few months and many people still do not even know who I am. I have done some really good things since I have been here, but it does not seem like anyone has noticed."
2. "Mr. Rice, the vice president, tells me I should be concentrating on reducing overhead, but then the regional managers yell at me because they are feeling squeezed from every side. I know that if they all just let me do my job, I would be able to find a good solution. Instead, it seems like everyone wants me to do things his way and then nothing gets done."
3. "Every day it's the same thing. First, I get all of the calculations from the previous day and then I summarize them for the marketing department. I could be doing this in my sleep."

4. "For the last few months things have really sucked because every deal I have brokered has fallen through. I just want to see one sale through from beginning to end—is that too much to ask?"
5. "This vendor has really screwed us over. It has been late with deliveries and then sometimes when we get the merchandise it's damaged and so we have to send it back. Over the last eighteen months, this has happened four times! I don't want to have to take the blame for all of this lost revenue, but I am afraid that is what will happen."

How to Use Vision Questions

Once you have determined which of your customer's needs is not being met, you can use that information to tailor vision questions for him. Let us go back to the chapter on impact questions for an example. In Chapter 6, the vice president of a chain of department stores lamented, "If we continue to lose money like this, I can't imagine I would be able to keep my job for much longer. I don't know what I would do if that happened." It is obvious from this statement that the vice president needs to feel a sense of security that he is not currently experiencing. Now that you are aware of this fact, you can use it to create a vision question just for him.

Vision Questions for a Customer Seeking Security

- "If you and I could find a solution to this problem, what affect do you think that would have on the company in the next five years?"
- "If you came to your boss with a solution that would save the company nearly $2 million per year, what would that mean to you?"
- "If those changes in your career were to happen now, how do you think your life would look five years from now?"

As you can see, vision questions are not overly complicated. They simply ask the customer to look to the future and imagine how great a change could be. Once you have gotten a customer to the point at which you will use a vision question, you have earned the right to convince her how your product or service can help achieve that goal.

Let us use the examples from the exercise earlier in this chapter to practice creating this type of question:

Exercise 2

After reading the examples, formulate a series of vision questions specific to the customer's implicit need. The first one has been done for you (see "Answer").

1. "I'm fairly new to this plant and starting to get to know some of the people here. I've implemented some changes but my boss doesn't seem to take notice."
2. "I'm pulled in so many directions, I can't even think straight. If everyone would just let me do my job!"
3. "I'm putting out the same old fires. Nothing changes. I'd rather spend my time with my customers."
4. "Every one of the last ten quotes have fallen through. What's it going to take to win some business?"
5. "My boss is on me to reduce the turnover in this department. Otherwise, I may be the next guy to go."

Answer

Answers to statement 1:

- "In our discussion we have calculated that using the new assembly line could save the company $1 million over the next two years. What impact would that have on your company?"
- "If you were able to save the company $1 million and pave the way for a new plant in Phoenix, how do you think you would be perceived at your company?"
- "What would it mean to you personally?"

Other Uses for Vision Questions

Vision questions do not only serve as the second half of impact questions. They can be used by themselves when it seems that a customer has already come to the Have To stage of commitment and does not need to be convinced with impact questions. Likewise, vision questions can be a way to salvage a conversation in which impact questions were not as effective as they should have been. Furthermore, generalized vision questions can be used during other parts of a meeting to determine the motivations of a customer. For example, sometimes customers are not as free in expressing their frustrations and concerns as those in the above exercises. A customer who seems standoffish and aloof might open up if asked a vision question.

Let's take an example. Our salesperson, Jeff, has been meeting for an excruciatingly long hour with Sandra, a prospective customer. Although Jeff has used educational questions, expansion questions, and lock-on questions, Sandra has yet to really open up and engage Jeff in conversation. Jeff is ready to throw in the towel and call it a day because he feels like he has not gotten anywhere with this sale, but he decides to ask one more question before he leaves.

Jeff: Sandra, I realize you are a very busy woman . . . let me ask you a question. Imagine yourself three years from today and you are looking back on those past three years. What will make you happy knowing that you accomplished something during this time frame?

Sandra: In three years I really hope to have moved up from divisional manager to vice president.

Jeff: What steps do you think you will need to take in order to move up to that position?

Sandra: Well, I have excellent performance reviews as well as four years' experience as a divisional manager, but I need to find a way to really make a dent in the bottom line.

Jeff: As you know, I have gathered data from your people and done extensive research into how we could save you money. Based on that data, I know that my service could save you almost $3 million a year in shipping fees. If you were to bring that kind of savings to your superiors, how would that help you attain your three-year goal?

Sandra: Hmmm, that's an interesting proposition. I was not aware that the savings could be that dramatic. If what you are saying is correct, I would be stupid not to present this idea. Let's see if I can arrange a meeting with the president next Tuesday morning. Is there any chance you could be there?

Some More Vision Questions

- "If you were able to achieve your goal, in what ways would it benefit the organization? How would it benefit your department? How would it benefit you personally?"
- "What is your vision for the future of your company [department, team, territory]? What do you see as the key steps you will need to take in order to get you there?"
- "What is your dream for the future of your career? What will you have to accomplish in order to get where you want to be?"
- "Try to picture yourself three years from now. Share with me exactly what has to happen in order for you to be satisfied with your progress."
- "What bothersome task could you stop doing if this problem were solved? What would you do with your free time?"
- "If you could accomplish your objective, what would that mean to you?"
- "If this problem were solved, what would it enable you to do?"

There are no downsides to using vision questions because of the positive tone and upbeat message they present. On a typical day, most of the working population remains locked in the present and does not think about the future and what it might bring for them. If you can use vision questions to lift your customers out of the present and into a sunny future, they will be forever grateful to you, not to mention the fact that they will almost certainly want to do business with you.

Getting Past "What If?" Objections and Stalls

NOT ALL SALES INTERACTIONS run smoothly, and sometimes as salespeople we hit a bump in the road. These bumps may be because of our own mishandling of a situation, or they may arise because of a customer's conflicted feelings about a sale. Either way, if we want to salvage our hard work and make sure that the sale goes through, we need to learn to deal with these obstacles so that the customer's needs are met.

The first step in this recovery process should be to uncover the real reasons behind a customer's objections or stalling tactics. It is only after you have discovered a customer's motivation for putting off the sale that you can begin to diffuse the situation. Once you know the reasons behind the objections, you can begin to create solutions that will soothe your customer's mind and protect the time you have invested in this sale.

You must be vigilant about your behavior during this process or you risk alienating a customer and losing a sale. The first part of this chapter will tell you about the most common mistakes salespeople make when encountering stalls. After you have learned how *not* to react to a customer's objections, you can go on to the following parts, which provide specific correct procedures for resolving customers' concerns.

The Mistakes Salespeople Make

There are six common mistakes that salespeople make when they encounter a customer's objection or stalling tactic:

1. **Fearing the customer's reaction.** Many salespeople are afraid of what a customer might say and they end up losing a sales opportunity because they do not discover what the customer really wants. For example, a salesperson dreads hearing the words, "Your price is too high." It's almost a knee-jerk reaction to respond with a lower price. Instead, a salesperson should be proactive and try to uncover the unique buying criteria important to the customer so the price objection would never come up in the first place.

2. **Taking it personally.** Although in our heads we know that a customer's bad attitude does not reflect on our worthiness as human beings, sometimes our egos get in the way and we internalize a customer's negativity. When a customer brings up a problem, this is not the time to get defensive and explain the problem away. Not only will the customer probably not be too thrilled with your response, but you will have failed to address the heart of the matter: what you can do to fix the customer's problem.

3. **Rushing to judgment.** As salespeople we should work to focus all of our attention on the customer and her needs. However, sometimes we fail in this pursuit. Instead of listening to a customer's complaints and the specifics of her situation, we swoop in to present our solution. In this rush to cut to the chase, we come across as arrogant and the customer ends up feeling that her input is not important.

   There are two reasons we make this mistake: (a) We want to be the "expert" and show off all of our knowledge by providing the solution before the customer even has a chance to finish a thought, or (b) we are in a hurry and do not have the time and energy to devote to the customer. Here's an example:

   Suppose you are getting ready to leave for a week of vacation when a prospective customer calls. He starts to go into a long-winded story about his business and all of the problems he has encountered in the last five years. You realize that you have heard his story many times before, and so you interrupt him to give your answer to his problems. You try to end the call as soon as possible so you can leave for vacation. In this case, even though you might have given the prospective customer a good solution, chances are he will not feel satisfied with the conversation. He did not have an opportunity to tell you about his business and he feels shortchanged. What should you have done?

Well, you need to embrace any information your prospective customer gives you, whether you believe it is valuable or not. If you truly did not have the time to talk at length with this prospect, you should have requested the opportunity to call him back after your vacation. Otherwise, you should have put down your briefcase, closed your office door, and listened to him for as long as he needed. Remember, even if you hear the story all the time, it is unique and personal for each customer. So, rather than interrupt the customer with your standard solution, let him have the stage and explain the problem. Only then can you get on with the process of finding a solution for whatever ails him.

4. **Beating a dead horse.** We all have customers who take up too much of our time. They provide us with little or no business, and yet they are demanding and even confrontational. Sometimes customers like this cost us money because we spend so much time trying to please them. We continue to do business with them in the hope that maybe, someday, they will reward us for our loyalty. What we need to realize is that there are some customers we just do not want! Whether it is a prospect who continues to string you along or a customer who demands to speak to you whenever the smallest problem arises, there are times when you have to make the difficult decision to terminate one-sided relationships.

    A customer of mine who manufacturers parts for one of the Big Three automotive companies was asked to meet 10 percent annual price concessions with the lure of becoming a valuable partner in the future. After the fourth year of price reductions, my customer realized that he did not want this kind of partner who could eventually drive his business under! So it is for you. Even though it may sound counterproductive, each year you should examine your customer list and fire the bottom 10 percent of your customers. Doing this frees up valuable time and allows you to focus on those customers and prospects who appreciate what you have to offer.

5. **Shifting blame.** For the past twenty years, organizations have embraced the concept of teamwork. When things go awry, though, it is easy to point fingers. Donald Trump's show, *The Apprentice*, really brings to life how individuals can turn on each other in order to protect their own self-interests. In that show, the boardroom meeting with "the Donald" shows a different side of the contestants' characters. One individual must be eliminated from the show each week, and so one individual is usually singled out for letting the team down.

When a customer comes to you with a problem about service, quality, price, or any other matter, do you know someone on your team who tries to shift blame to another person or department in your company? Pointing fingers in this way will only delay the inevitable: resolving the issue your customer is facing. When things go well in your organization you should definitely share the glory. When things go wrong, however, responsibility should also be shared.

6. **Treating all customer complaints with the same approach.** Some salespeople have a one-size-fits-all approach when it comes to dealing with customer objections. They may offer to lower their price by 5 percent or throw in some product extras automatically, without listening to the reasons the customer is upset. While you are being conditioned to respond to objections with concessions, your customers are learning that whenever they complain they are rewarded. For example, a customer might ask you to reduce your price by 5 percent in order to clinch a deal. When you agree to this deal you are setting up her expectations for the next time you negotiate. She will think that all she has to do is raise an objection and you will give in once again.

There are two reasons that having only one approach to resolving customer issues is a mistake: You are not addressing the customer's real problem and oftentimes you offer more than what the customer really wants. Instead of giving all stalling customers a 5 percent price reduction to close the deal, listen to what the customer tells you and then go from there.

Now that we have examined the problems salespeople often encounter when dealing with customer objections, we need to learn why customers object at all. It is important to know why the customer acts in these ways in order to overcome these objections and move on with the sale.

The Motives for Stalling

Why do customers bring up objections to your proposals and use stalling tactics? Customers, just like salespeople, have hopes and fears for their jobs and their lives. As I discussed in the previous chapters, customer motivation comes from various sources, which include internal customers, external customers, career goals, performance pressures, and competition. All of these factors operate within a customer's mind as he is deciding whether or not to do business with you. Here are some of the main customer motives for stalling or raising objections:

- **"What if it doesn't work?"** Almost 100 percent of the customers you will deal with worry about their reputations and their jobs. If they approve of a sale and then the product or service does not perform as promised, they will look foolish and might even get fired! Everyone has gotten stuck with a lemon at one time or another. Buyer's remorse never really goes away and anytime we make a big purchase we worry about the possibility that our money will go to waste.

  Customers buying for their companies are much more cautious today than they were thirty years ago. The volatile economy and the lack of loyalty at most large companies cause many managers to simply avoid making a decision so that they cannot be blamed if something goes wrong.

- **"You're an outsider."** Many customers are very territorial about their businesses. They do not want to see someone from the outside coming in and getting all of the attention and glory. Have you ever given a suggestion to improve a product or service in your own organization? Usually the suggestion will get tabled and then somewhere down the line it will get "tweaked" by someone else. Your suggestion gets implemented and the other person gets all the glory! This is a feeling that does not go away, and it makes customers especially suspicious of outsiders.

  As a consultant I use being an outsider to my advantage. I have worked with thousands of organizations and have the ability to see the bigger picture while the customers are caught up in the minutiae of day-to-day business. Even though I have these experiences, I am the first to acknowledge that the best ideas often come from inside an organization. Most companies fail to listen to the suggestions and problems of their own people. The input of internal customers is often treated like noise rather than invaluable advice. Internal customers crave the spotlight, however, and want to be able to wow others in the organization. As an outsider you have the opportunity to not only bring fresh eyes to the situation but also give an internal customer the chance to be a hero by bringing an outstanding proposal to the table.

- **"I just don't get it."** All companies must abide by budgets; our customers are no exception. Sometimes, however, people become obsessed with the bottom line and forget about the big picture. Even if you have done your job, have demonstrated what it's costing them in their current situation and illustrated how much money the company will save in the long run, some customers will simply resist spending any money. Some people simply lack vision and live their whole lives reacting rather than proacting. When you ask them what their long-term goals are, they do not have a clue or they can think ahead only as far as the weekend. Many others simply lack the confidence to initiate solutions to their problems.

A customer will never admit that he does not have the confidence to make a decision; instead, he will mask this fear with statements such as, "I am concerned," "I am not ready," or "I do not feel comfortable." As a salesperson you will need to use your professional judgment to determine whether this person can be motivated to change or if you need to find another contact in the company.

- **"I just don't like you."** It is inevitable that we will encounter customers we do not get along with or with whom we have no connection. If, for example, you are a fast-paced and decisive individual, you might have trouble dealing with a customer who likes to take things slow and mull over decisions. In this instance, you will inevitably clash with the customer. When this happens, it is easy for the customer to get wrapped up in the personality conflict while disregarding your product or service. This type of customer might even bad-mouth you to others in the company, simply because you and she do not get along. It is your responsibility as a professional to recognize when a conflict such as this arises and adapt your approach accordingly.

Whatever the reason behind a customer's objection, it is your job as a salesperson to discover that reason and then deal with it! The next section will provide you with the tools to do just that.

The Four-Step Process for Handling Objections

The following process will give you the ability to deal with any and all customer objections and stalls. This does not mean that a sale will always result; there are times when customers are just not ready to do business, no matter what you say or do. But by using this process, you will be able to not only unearth the motive for an objection but also determine if the objection can be overcome.

Step 1: Find a Point of Agreement

No matter what the customer's objection, you can always find some point of agreement that you can then latch onto. (Note: This is very similar to the Clarifying step in the qualifying process discussed in Chapter 3.) When customers make provocative statements such as, "Your price is just too high," they expect salespeople to counter their statements, or even argue with them. Instead of doing that, however, find some element of their statements with which you can agree. Once you have done that, move on to the next phase of the process.

Step 2: Offer a Question to Clarify

Your customer will no doubt be taken aback that you have agreed with a statement of objection. This is a good thing because you can use that moment to ask a question about the situation at hand. You want to ask a question that will get to the heart of the customer's problem and lead to a successful conclusion.

Step 3: Educate the Customer

After you have given the customer a chance to vent her feelings and complain to you about the situation, you need to provide her with the reassurance that this problem can be overcome. This can be done by using one of the following methods:

- **Results.** A customer who seems to doubt your product might change her mind if you show her concrete results you have achieved with other companies. The facts should not come from you, but from a third party whom your customer knows to be objective and credible. Customers, while motivated by their emotions, justify their actions with logic.

- **Examples.** There are many customers who need to "see" things in order to understand them, whether it is a graph or a simulated picture of a future construction project. Seeing is believing, especially when dealing with generations X and Y, who have become focused on visual stimuli because they have grown up with MTV, video games, and the Internet.

Another way to provide examples is to share any past experience you have had, with other customers or in your own company, where a similar objection had been put to rest. Stories are some of the best examples you can use to convince customers. Have you ever received a solicitation in the mail to contribute to a charity that provides food and medical care to orphans? Inevitably the letter begins with a story about a specific child's experience and then details how this can be overcome with your contribution. The one child's story gives life to the thousands of others who share her plight. This is the power of examples.

* **Comparisons.** Sometimes our products might seem a little complicated to customers unfamiliar with the technology or jargon. Relating similar ideas on a lower level (for example, "Using this microchip is like putting a computer on fast-forward") often helps a customer grasp a difficult concept. Comparisons can set a customer's mind at ease and assure him that you are not trying to sell him something he doesn't need.

Once you have educated your customer about the situation, it is time to move to the final phase of this process.

Step 4: Secure a Commitment

In this last step you simply need to bring the conversation full circle. Now that you have diffused the situation and learned more about your customer's needs, you are that much more prepared to offer a solution. Return to the sale at hand and work out a plan that both you and your customer can feel good about.

*   *   *

Although there are four steps in this process, there may be times when it is not necessary to use all of them. If you learn information from your customer that indicates a sale cannot or will not happen, it is important to cut your losses and walk away. Many salespeople are reluctant to do this because they feel as if this makes them failures; however, this is not true. It would be a failure only if the salesperson realizes that there is no hope for the sale but keeps on pursuing it, to the detriment of his other customers. Though we salespeople do not like to hear it, sometimes a commitment will just never happen. In those cases, our time is better spent elsewhere.

These steps in the process might seem a little abstract and confusing right now, so let's look at several examples of how to use the process in everyday situations.

Use of the Four-Step Process

So many of the objections salespeople hear each day are the same. Customers either want you to lower your prices, increase the quality of your service, or leave them alone altogether because they cannot be bothered to think about your product. Here are examples of the most common scenarios, not so you can recite them word for word the next time a customer objects, but so you can learn the technique and adapt it to your personal style and preference.

Common Objections About Price

Many salespeople avoid questions about budget and price. They fear offending a customer or hearing an answer that they will not like. For example, they fear what will happen if they ask a customer, "What is your budget?" and they get a number that is too low. Or, a customer demands that they lower their price in order to continue with the process. Here are various questions and good responses about price and budget that will eliminate these fears and anxieties:

- **Objection:** Your price is too high. *Point of Agreement:* I understand that money is an important issue to you. *Question to Clarify:* Can you share with me the criteria you use when choosing a vendor?

- **Objection:** There is no money in the budget. *Point of Agreement:* Well, I can certainly agree that managing your finances is crucial when doing business. *Questions to Clarify:* (1) Is it a budgetary concern or not being convinced of the value you will receive? (2) What will it take to secure funding so that you no longer have to experience the problem of [state a problem your customer shared with you to drive home the frustration of having to continue with his continuing situation]? (3) What would allow you to convince yourself that this is an important investment for you [and your organization], and not a cost? If the response is positive, ask, Then how can you go about securing the necessary funding to take advantage of this opportunity now versus later?

- **Objection:** Another vendor has offered us the same deal for 15 percent less. *Point of Agreement*: Getting the best value for your money is important. *Questions to Clarify*: (1) Tell me how important price is compared to quality [or on-time delivery, or service, or meeting customer expectations]. (2) Share with me the buying criteria you are using for evaluation purposes. (3) Tell me what's most important to you: getting the cheapest price or the lowest total cost? (4) It's important that you get the most for your investment. Could you share with me your decision-making criteria? (5) What if this product/service could give you a _____ percent ROI. Would price still be an issue? (6) What if I were to go back to my managers and they were to agree to that price? Would you do business with me? Emphasize the "what if"—make it clear you are not committing, only that you are trying to determine if it's really a price concern or something else. The last thing you want to do is to lower your price and not get the business.

Still More Questions to Clarify Price

- "Could you describe for me your budgetary process?"
- "So that I can tailor the right solution, what budgetary parameters are you working within?"
- "How will the funding for this project be determined?"
- "How will you go about getting financial approval for this solution?"
- "What hurdles might you encounter when trying to get financial commitment for this project?"
- "Who else will be involved in approving the budget?"
- "On a scale of 1 to 10, how important will it be to get the service/product implemented?"
- "What kind of return on investment are you expecting?"

General Objections Aimed at Stalling

If you recall the stages of commitment discussed earlier in the book, stalls are nothing more than customers in the Should or Want To stage. Your goal is to uncover the hot button or motive that will get them to the Have To stage.

- **Objection:** I need to think about it. *Point of Agreement*: I am glad you are going to give this careful consideration. *Question to Clarify*: What are some of the things you like about what I have said so far, and what things do you have concerns about?

- **Objection:** We have too much going on right now. *Point of Agreement*: Making sure your time, energy, and resources are invested wisely is important. *Question to Clarify*: What will help you make this a priority?

- **Objection:** We are not ready to move forward. *Point of Agreement*: I understand your reluctance to make a big decision such as this one. *Question to Clarify*: Do you think you could help me understand what is causing your hesitation?

Objections with You (or the Company)

Many times objections are ambiguous. Get the customer to be specific and you'll be able to isolate what the real concern is.

- **Objection:** We are unhappy with your service. *Point of Agreement*: Getting your needs met is essential in any business relationship. *Question to Clarify*: In what ways have we not been meeting your expectations?

- **Objection:** We like our current vendor. *Point of Agreement*: Receiving the best quality, support, and service for your business is extremely important. *Question to Clarify*: Walk me through your decision-making criteria for choosing a vendor.

- **Objection:** You just do not understand our business. *Point of Agreement*: It is vital that any vendor know as much as possible about your situation. *Question to Clarify*: Could you share with me the problems you have been experiencing or the areas in which you have concerns?

Now that you've had plenty of examples, it's your turn to practice reacting to some objections on your own:

Exercise

1. Objection: "The last shipment we ordered from you was over two weeks late. We won't ever order from you again!" Identify the point of agreement. What question will you ask to clarify?

2. Objection: "Management has been cracking down on spending. There have been virtually no funds allocated for this fiscal year." Identify the point of agreement. What is your question to clarify?

3. Objection: "I am not the one making the decision; it will be made by the committee." Identify the point of agreement. What will you ask to clarify?

4. Objection: "Your prices are twice as high as Company X's!" Identify the point of agreement. What will you ask to clarify?

5. Objection: "Your company is too small. We only deal with the big fish." Identify the point of agreement. What question will you ask to clarify?

6. Objection: "I called your support line last week and was on hold for forty-five minutes!" Identify the point of agreement. What will you ask to clarify?

7. Objection: "There won't be any decisions about that until the beginning of the year." Identify the point of agreement. What will you ask to clarify?

*   *   *

The examples in this chapter have given you some ideas about the way this process works. In many ways, it is so simple: Rather than assume you know what the customer is thinking or feeling, you just ask! Once you have constructed a great question, you need only listen to the answer to discover what ails your customer. After that, you can educate the customer about how your product or service can alleviate that pain. Then all that is left is for you to close the deal.

Putting It All Together

THIS BOOK HAS INTRODUCED YOU to numerous tools you can use to increase the quality of your business interactions and build real relationships with your customers. Now you will practice using those tools together. As you go through the exercises in this chapter, notice that there are no hard-and-fast rules regulating the order of questions; for example, you might find that opening with an educational question will work in some instances but not others. The key to using these questions lies in listening to the customers and then responding to their concerns, ideas, and frustrations.

Instead of using an example of one of the salespeople introduced in previous chapters, this chapter focuses on you. You will be the salesperson navigating the business situation, creating questions appropriate for the customer. I have chosen a scenario that is simple and generic: automobiles. This choice allows you to focus on the engagement process instead of having to acquire product knowledge.

The purpose of this book has been to help you in your business-to-business selling. This final scenario is a challenge, a way for you to use the questioning strategies presented here in a complex environment that includes multiple calls, several business personalities, and complex analysis. Your goals should be to obtain a genuine understanding of the company's decision-making process, the criteria used by key players in the company, and the motivating forces behind the customers' decisions. The lessons you will learn here can be applied to all fields of business.

The Scenario

Your company, Sheatler Financial, specializes in commercial leasing with an emphasis on providing motor vehicles to companies with outside sales, service, and technical support. Sheatler, like other companies in this industry, is a third-party leasing firm. The leasing industry faces the same challenges as other industries that are commodity driven: Customers shop for the best price.

Sheatler started only ten years ago and already competes with numerous third-party commercial leasing firms, as well as with leading financial institutions. Your company tries to distinguish itself from the competition by offering value-added solutions and superior service. As the sales agent in charge of commercial leasing, you have a good deal of sway in the industry and access to thousands of cars and trucks at a moment's notice.

Recently, you have done business with a real estate company that required vehicles for approximately fifty realtors, as well as a cosmetics company outfitting its sales representatives with purple luxury sedans. Today you received a memo from your boss concerning a scale company that needs trucks for hundreds of technicians throughout the United States. The scale company, Metro Scales, recently terminated its contract with another leasing firm that went out of business.

Here's the information your boss provided to you:

- Metro Scales, a Fortune 1000 company, is looking for a new contract for 3,000 trucks. The vice president of the company, Lou Tyler, drives a hard bargain. He has basically run the company for the last twenty-two years because the president would rather spend his days in Saint Tropez. The sales technicians are the heart of the company; they are the ones who install the scales and fix them when they break down. The technicians cannot get anywhere without their trucks. They rely on them not only to transport scales but also to test weights (to calibrate the scales) and tools.

- You need to find a contact in the company to get your foot in the door; otherwise, Sheatler Financial will be lost among the big-name competitors like Citibank, Wells Fargo, Wachovia, and Bank of America. Be careful not to step on anyone's toes because there has been talk of a merger between Metro Scales and another major scale company, which has made Metro's employees nervous.

Exercise 1

Prepare a list of questions for Vanessa O'Reilly, who is in charge of transportation for Metro Scales. She is the one who must deal with the technicians' complaints about breakdowns or other problems with reliability. If the trucks do not run smoothly, Vanessa is not happy. You have a phone meeting scheduled with Vanessa during which you hope not only to engage her but also to uncover some valuable information about her company's needs. This will probably be your only chance to get your foot in the door because your company is not as well known as the others who are competing for the contract. If you can get Vanessa on your side, however, you will have gone a long way toward completing this sale. In the spaces below, compile some possible questions to ask Vanessa in the upcoming meeting. (In the parentheses, you are reminded to include several different types of questions and address various business influences.)

1. (An expansion question that addresses internal customers)

   _____

   _____

2. (A question that uncovers performance pressures, such as reducing overhead, increasing profits, or constraints on the customer's time)

   _____

   _____

3. (A comparison question that addresses satisfaction with current vendors)

   _____

   _____

4. (A vision question that addresses goals for the company as well as Vanessa's career goals)

   _____

   _____

After talking with Vanessa, you have discovered the following things:

1. Vanessa is extremely unhappy with the current vendor and glad to see it go. The technicians constantly came to her with truck problems, complaining about having to take their vehicles in to be serviced and then missing out on overtime because they did not have access to a vehicle. She also complained that the current vendor was slow to get her new vehicles, sometimes taking up to six months to provide a truck to a new technician.

2. Upper management has put pressure on Vanessa consistently over the last two years because of lost productivity owing to all the needed repairs. Vanessa tried again and again to explain that the problem was with the trucks and not her, and after two years she was finally vindicated when the current vendor filed for bankruptcy.

3. The company was losing a good amount of money each year because of truck breakdowns and the time it took to repair them. Vanessa told you that, on average, three trucks break down each day (out of 3,000 trucks nationwide). This translates to fifteen trucks per week and fifteen technicians complaining to Vanessa. She estimated that she has to spend twelve hours per week to simply keep the trucks up and running, and keep one person in her office dedicating all her time to rescheduling appointments because of truck breakdowns.

4. Vanessa feels that Lou Tyler (the company's vice-president) has always respected her, but the chief of operations, Tim Daly, has often refused to acknowledge how central transportation is to Metro Scales's very survival. Rather than recognizing the importance of transportation, Daly focuses all of his energies on increasing productivity and reaching sales and service quotas.

5. The talk of merger around Metro Scales has reached a fever pitch and Vanessa fears her job might be downsized if the merger takes place.

Exercise 2

Using the information you have learned from Vanessa, construct impact questions that will highlight the problems of the current vendor.

1. Impact question #1 (Hint: impact on customers)

   _____

   _____

2. Impact question #2 (Hint: impact on the company)

   _____

   _____

3. Impact question #3 (Hint: impact on Vanessa and her ability to get
   her work done)

   _____

   _____

Owing to your insightful questions and engagement of Vanessa O'Reilly, you have been able to secure a "sit-down" with her and Tim Daly. The meeting will take place a week from today, so you need to gather information about the current state of affairs for the scale industry. You also need to formulate questions to ask Tim Daly so that you will be able to move the sale forward. From your research you have found that the scale industry has been growing steadily over the last several years, and Metro Scales has been doing relatively well.

Sales of new scales generally depend on the state of the economy. If businesses are doing well and expanding, then they buy new scales; if businesses are suffering, then they will put off buying new scales and just repair their old ones. Metro Scales also generates a good deal of revenue from its contracts—companies with a large number of scales often purchase a service contract that entitles them to service around the clock and a set rate for repairs.

As Vanessa O'Reilly told you, the scale business cannot function without trucks. Trucks get the technicians, their tools, and the scales to the customers. Customers, especially those with service contracts, want their scales fixed now! Excuses about trucks being repaired or, worse, not enough trucks for each technician ring hollow to customers who are losing money every minute their scales are out of commission.

After your initial meeting with Vanessa and your stellar use of the impact questions, Vanessa called you with more precise information. She told you that a full 5 percent of customer calls currently require rescheduling because of truck problems. Each technician has approximately 120 customers, and on average each customer is worth $20,000 per year to Metro Scales. (This is great information to use in order to quantify the problem.)

Now that you have all of this information at your disposal, you need to formulate some possible questions for Tim Daly, chief of operations. Daly's main responsibilities include supervision of the ten regional managers and keeping an eye on the bottom line. Vanessa has told you that Daly responds to numbers, especially those with dollar signs in front of them.

Exercise 3

Prepare your questions for Tim Daly, chief of operations. Remember to use the information you learned from Vanessa, as well as from your own research.

1. An expansion question dealing with the bottom line (Hint: This would include such areas as employee productivity, sales quotas, and the amount of time technicians spend with each of their customers.)

   _____

   _____

2. A comparison question addressing expectations of a vendor (Hint: comparing its current experience with an ideal one.)

   _____

   _____

3. A qualifying or comparison question concerning the decision-making process (Hint: Try to uncover the different sets of buying criteria among the decision makers.)

   _____

   _____

4. An expansion or comparison question related to external customers (Hint: This is a great opportunity to create a sense of urgency by shining the light on the qualities customers want from Metro Scales but are not currently getting. The information you gather will lead you to the next question when you quantify the problem and its impact on the company.)

_____

_____

5. A question that quantifies the problem (Hint: Focus on how the problem is negatively affecting Metro Scales.)

_____

_____

6. A vision question

_____

_____

As you prepare for your meeting with Tim Daly, you call him to determine if there are any particular areas of concern that he would like you to address during your presentation. He tells you, "I want to see an increase in profit by 10 percent over the next quarter and I do not want to have to worry about transportation—this should not have to be my major concern."

Exercise 4

Use Tim Daly's statement to construct lock-on questions. You should be able to write at least four lock-on questions from this one statement. I have given you an example to help jog your memory.

Example: Tim, you mentioned that you want to see an increase in profit by 10 percent. Do you find that others in the company share your vision or has there been some disagreement as to short- and long-term goals?

1. _____

_____

_____

2. _____
    _____
    _____

3. _____
    _____
    _____

4. _____
    _____
    _____

After meeting with Tim Daly, you are buoyed by the impact you appear to have made on this tough-to-please businessman. Here is what you have found out:

1. The company has been losing a lot of money without realizing it. Tim estimated that the company has 360,000 customers across the nation. You related Vanessa's information that 5 percent of calls had to be rescheduled and you calculated that this translates to 18,000 unhappy customers per year. Tim commented that probably 10 percent of those 18,000 customers (which is 1,800 customers) leave every year and go to Metro Scales's competition because of scheduling delays; together you computed a total loss of $36 million per year (when an average customer is worth $20,000 per year). This was eye-opening for Tim Daly!

2. Although Tim did not really appreciate the problems Vanessa and the technicians were encountering with the current vendor, he did recognize how the company's productivity was suffering because of these problems. When he learned that fifteen technicians each week were sitting around waiting for their trucks to be repaired, he was furious! He estimated this issue alone cut into productivity and cost Metro Scales $2 million a year.

3. In your meeting with Vanessa and Tim, Vanessa commented that the current vendor's trucks were getting only 16 miles per gallon. Metro Scales is currently spending $9 million each year on gas for its technicians.

4. After encouraging Tim to share his worries with you, he revealed that Metro Scales was falling short of its sales and service quotas by nearly 15 percent. He also told you that Lou Tyler, the company's vice president, had recently questioned him about this problem.

Now you are getting the golden opportunity: the chance to meet with Lou Tyler and convince him of the worthiness of Sheatler Financial and what it can do for Metro Scales. During your meeting with Lou you will need to do a couple of things:

• Summarize all of the numbers and calculations you have learned from talking with Vanessa and Tim. Remember to lay out all of the ways Metro Scales has been losing money by dealing with the current vendor. Highlight the ways that Sheatler Financial could reduce and/or eliminate these losses and therefore increase Metro Scales's profits.

• Take Lou through another series of impact questions, this time dealing with the issue of spending on gas for the trucks. Inform Lou that Sheatler has access to new trucks with a gas mileage of 24 miles per gallon, which could save him on average $3 million each year.

• Disclose the fact that your company's leasing services will cost Metro Scales 25 percent more each year than it was paying its current vendor, but be sure to remind Lou of the savings he will derive from your company and that the net gain will be millions of dollars.

Exercise 5

This is the ultimate test of your skills. You will be talking to the vice president of the company—the person empowered to make a final decision about the sale. Ensure that your questions not only illustrate how much money the company is losing right now because of its current leasing contract but also how much money the company stands to gain by doing business with Sheatler Financial.

1. Provide a series of impact questions dealing with gas mileage and how it is affecting Metro Scales's bottom line.

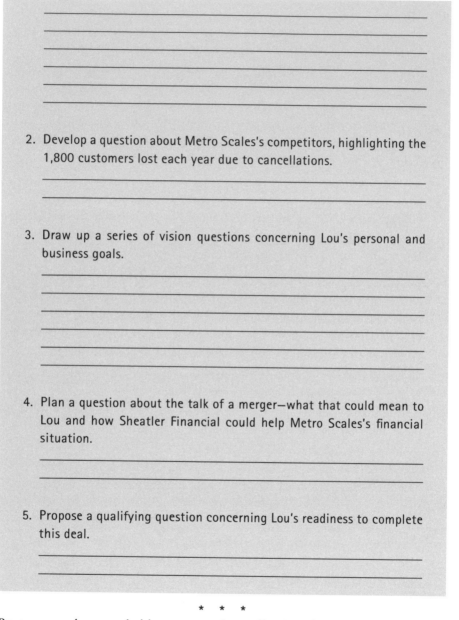

2. Develop a question about Metro Scales's competitors, highlighting the 1,800 customers lost each year due to cancellations.

3. Draw up a series of vision questions concerning Lou's personal and business goals.

4. Plan a question about the talk of a merger—what that could mean to Lou and how Sheatler Financial could help Metro Scales's financial situation.

5. Propose a qualifying question concerning Lou's readiness to complete this deal.

* * *

By now you have probably come to the realization that this type of selling does not eliminate all complications. There are still problems that could arise and personal matters that might interfere with the sale. But you have all of these tools at your disposal, and you should be able to anticipate any objections, alleviate any fears, and motivate your customers to make a decision. Whether you use an educational question, an impact question, or a qualifying question, you'll find that, after practice using these techniques, you will certainly have an edge over your competition.

CHAPTER

Conclusion

I HOPE THAT YOU have learned a lot from the strategies presented in this book. By using the techniques offered here, you will be able to establish and maintain more meaningful relationships with your customers. According to Claude Lévi-Strauss, a famous anthropologist of the twentieth century, "The wise man doesn't give the right answers, he poses the right questions." I named this book *Questions That Sell* because I sincerely believe that selling is about what you ask, not what you say.

It might seem at first as if you are going through your professional life constantly asking questions. I assure you that will not be the case. The beauty of asking questions is that you are prompting the other person to do most of the talking. Once you have posed a few, well-thought-out questions, your customers will have much information they will wish to share with you. Your responsibility at that point is to listen carefully to their answers, and respond with questions only when appropriate. It might be a struggle at first to let your customers do so much talking, but ultimately their words will help you provide them with the most viable solution.

This book provides all of the tools you need to cultivate such beneficial relationships. Now that you have read the book, you know what your clients need from you. They do not want a product peddler or someone who will provide a one-size-fits-all approach. Your clients want a salesperson who can provide expertise and an individualized plan. Educational questions, comparison questions, expansion questions, and lock-on questions all enable you to dig deeper to uncover your clients' needs and wants. When you can tailor your services to the desires of your clients, you are performing an invaluable service—one your customers will not soon forget.

By providing such tailor-made solutions, you will be bringing greater value to your client. Customers love to get more value for their money, and this is exactly what they get from someone using these techniques. Remember, your expertise and experience can bring worth to the table.

Another important lesson in this book is the practice of self-evaluation. I asked you to do this in the beginning, when you wrote down the questions you would typically ask a prospective client. You were then supposed to call a prospect and take notes on how far your questions went in establishing a beneficial relationship. This practice of self-evaluation should be something you do constantly, not just once in a book. If you notice that things at work are going particularly well, take a moment to evaluate what you are doing correctly and examine why it is working. If you have been having a tough couple of weeks, also sit down and make a list of the things that have not been working for you. Either way, assess your performance and look for ways to improve it.

In the end, that is what this book is about. If it were possible, I would come to the workplace of each of my readers in order to help them establish better relationships with their customers. Unfortunately, I do not have the time or the frequent flier miles to accomplish such a task. This book is the next best thing. You can read about my techniques and then individualize them for yourself, taking the best of what I have to offer and combining it with the best of what makes you an already successful salesperson. Good luck in your journey!

Show Me the Money!
How to Create Value so
Price Is No Longer an Issue

In Chapter 6, dealing with lock on questions, I address the notion of quantifying the costs for customers in order to illustrate how much money they are currently wasting or will be wasting if they do not do business with you. This process allows you not only to demonstrate how much money you can save your customers but also alleviates their concerns about spending money on your particular product or service. I provided a few examples of areas you might address when dealing with various customers; however, I recognize that it is not always easy to uncover where a customer's money is being spent. Therefore, I include this appendix to further illuminate the various avenues you can take to justify why someone should do business with you.

I have also widened the scope of the industries discussed to include construction, manufacturing, health care, food production, and customer service/technical support. I hope that by providing specifics for each of these industries I will cover most of the ways in which you can create value for your product or service.

Why do I spend so much time on this? So many of the salespeople I advise have expressed the same frustration: "I'm selling the highest-price solution. What can I do to establish value in my customer's eyes?"

Getting customers to realize the value of your solution begins with asking the right questions. In order to do this, you need to identify your customers' typical costs and then decide whether or not they could be reduced or eliminated through use of your product or service. Figure A-1 is a chart with a fairly extensive list of common expenses. Peruse this list and check off those expenses that you could explore with your customers. I have also included specific examples of how to quantify costs for their current situation, which will stimulate your critical thinking and prompt you to discover areas ripe for your own industry.

Health Care

Outsourcing has become a hot topic among businesspeople and politicians in the last few years, and many of my clients ask me my opinion of it. I certainly understand the compulsion to use lower-wage workers abroad who have the same skills as workers at home. I always worry, though, about the unforeseen consequences of such actions. Remember, I tell my clients, if you want to employ individuals in another country, you have to expect the unexpected.

One of my clients sells hospital equipment. He casually mentioned to me one day that several local hospitals were considering outsourcing radiol-

FIGURE A-1. Common expenses cited in quantifying costs.

Initial costs			
Design	Production	Equipment	Recruitment/ training
Labor costs			
Salary for personnel involved	Benefits for additional personnel	Turnover costs	Additional office space for new personnel
Quality costs			
Preventative costs: reducing or eliminating defects	Cost to correct defects (lost production time)	Litigation costs to cover lawsuits due to defects	Cost to replace defective products (lost profit)
Availability costs			
Acquisition costs (processing orders, issuing purchasing orders, receiving and handling materials)	Possession costs (include storage, insurance, taxes, and maintenance)	Delivery costs (rush shipping because item not in stock, overtime to handlers, spoiled merchandise)	Customer relations (customers taking their business elsewhere, penalties for late deliveries)

ogy positions to doctors in other parts of the world. I was intrigued by this development and asked him to explain. He said that for years hospitals had struggled during the night shift to find radiologists available to read x-rays in emergencies. At first, a different radiologist would be on call each night, and when an x-ray needed to be read, this doctor would be paged and would have to drive to the hospital from his home.

With the advent of e-mail, hospitals began sending x-rays to local doctors electronically. The radiologists, however, quickly tired of this practice because it meant that they had to be near a computer all night and had to incessantly check their e-mail. These local hospitals had since been contacted by an international agency that employed radiologists licensed to practice in the United States (but currently living abroad), who would spend their workdays reading x-rays sent to them by American hospitals. So, in the middle of the night on the East Coast, a hospital would send an x-ray of an emergency patient and it would be read by a doctor in Berlin, Hong Kong, or Calcutta. The agency would charge a flat fee each month, which would allow the hospital to save approximately $500,000 per year. My client asked me what I thought of this prospect.

Before I tell you what I think, I want you to take a minute and think about the situation. What do you think of this idea? Would you be ready to counsel your customers to make a deal such as this? Your customers would probably be excited to hear that they could save half a million dollars each year, but are there any hidden costs that might surprise a customer later on?

Let us look at some of the pros and cons to help identify the areas you could address:

Pros

- The first, and the most obvious, the customer will save $500,000 each year.

- Hospital patients will be served more quickly because their x-rays will be read instantly. They will not have to wait for an on-call radiologist to check his e-mail and read the x-rays.

- Each hospital will be able to eliminate three radiologists from its staff. Not only will this save money (see above), but each hospital will now have additional office space available for the nurses who desperately need it.

Cons

- Possible effects to the doctors' malpractice insurance. Even though the agency claims that its doctors are U.S. board certified, how can your customers be sure? Will the insurance company that carries the doctors' malpractice insurance object to this new practice? Or, will the malpractice premium simply be raised because of this increased risk?

- What happens if the Internet goes down? If the hospital is relying on doctors overseas (instead of those on the other side of town), there is no recourse if the connection fails. Prior to this change, doctors could come in to the hospital and read the x-rays if the computer was not working. What would happen now, when there are no local doctors on call?

- A lack of rapport between patient and doctor. How would patients feel if they could not interact with the doctor who reads their x-rays? What if a patient has questions about the diagnosis—who will answer them?

- Where is the accountability? If there is a mistake, who will take responsibility for it? The hospital would now have to assume liability for doctors whom it has never interviewed and never met.

- Issues of confidentiality must be considered. In the past few years laws have been passed that carefully guard the privacy of all patients. What effects might transmitting x-rays overseas have on privacy rights? Could the system be vulnerable to hackers?

Although there do seem to be advantages to this scheme, I found that the risks possibly outweighed the benefits. As I went through this process, it provided me with several avenues to explore. This is the type of thinking you can do when evaluating the costs of a given situation.

Health-Care Cost Justification

The following are things to consider to validate costs in the health-care industry:

- Reimbursements and medicare payments
- Malpractice litigation
- Quality of care—caliber of doctors and nurses
- Personnel costs—salary and benefits

- Equipment costs—medical equipment such as x-ray machines and basic office equipment like computers and faxes
- Government regulations
- Patient satisfaction
- Patient confidentiality—whether there are paper files or electronic transmissions
- Usable space fees—cost to house equipment and personnel
- Training costs—the money and time needed to familiarize personnel with new systems and equipment
- Start-up costs—the money and time needed to implement a new program
- Operational costs—service expenses, replacement and replenishing costs

Construction

Selling bricks is not all that exciting, but it is possible to quantify costs. Jackie sells bricks to home owners building new houses and construction companies creating new neighborhoods. It is difficult to convince either of these parties to use bricks because they are more expensive than other building materials. Jackie has found a great way to market her bricks to both home owners and construction companies. She simply presents each side with some facts:

- Bricks hold heat better than other materials, so in the long run you will save on heating bills.
- Unlike siding, which needs to be replaced after years of wear and tear, bricks last a lifetime.
- Studies have shown that, all other things being equal, a brick house will sell for 15 percent more than a house with siding.
- For construction companies, bricks are easier to work with and easier to store than other materials.

Although these all seem like simple ideas, put together they really make a difference. Jackie has watched as her sales increased by 25 percent after she started using a cost justification system. Prior to this change, Jackie had struggled because bricks were so much more expensive than other building materials. When home owners and contractors asked her why they should use this more expensive material, she used to have nothing to say. Therefore, Jackie's sales had been limited to high-end houses and home owners who really wanted brick. Now she has been able to hire two new workers and expand her business simply by creating value in the eyes of her customers.

Construction Cost Justification

The following are things to remember when quantifying construction costs:

- Cost to acquire, store, and deliver materials
- Labor costs (wages, benefits, and training)
- Training and recruiting costs
- Resale value
- Customer satisfaction (if the customer is not satisfied, bad word of mouth will probably spread)
- Equipment and maintenance costs
- Costs of possible delays (overtime, penalties for late completion, wasted man-hours waiting for deliveries)

Manufacturing

Although customers do not always believe salespeople, there are many times when we can see things they cannot. As outsiders we have that advantage. I cannot count how many times I have tried to warn a client against doing something that I knew would cost him money, but he did it anyway. Sometimes our customers can be very stubborn; once they make a decision, they do not want to hear any of the negative consequences that might occur. But it is as outsiders that we can bring value to our customer relationships.

Let us look at another example: Lois runs a motorcycle assembly plant in the Midwest. The plant customizes motorcycles for stores throughout the country; it is a small but lucrative operation. Lois has decided to switch from the traditional model of production to the just-in-time system. She assumes that she will save money on storage fees and will no longer lose money buying large quantities of parts that will never be used. Instead of keeping a large quantity of parts in stock, the plant will now order only those parts that are needed at that moment.

As an outsider looking in on Lois's company, I see the potential pitfalls involved in this switch. Here are my areas of concern:

- Just-in-time operations work well when everything runs smoothly, but that rarely happens. If Lois orders a part and her regular provider does not have it in stock, what will she do? If she waits to get the part, she risks losing the customer's business. If she orders from another, unfamiliar supplier, the part might not be of the same quality. Either way, Lois risks losing the customer because the desired part is not in stock.

- More and more deliveries coming into the United States are subject to searches. Lois often orders parts from a distributor in South America. There have been three instances in the past year when a container bound for Lois was hung up at customs for more than a week. If Lois were to become dependent on this type of delivery, she makes herself vulnerable to the uncertainties of the U.S. Customs Agency.

- Labor disputes are another concern. If workers were to go on strike, the port could shut down. A hurricane or a natural disaster is yet another factor to take into consideration.

- Overtime costs could increase drastically if Lois does not always have the parts she needs on hand. If any of the above delivery problems occur, the plant will have to work overtime to produce the motorcycle and send it to the customer. Not only could her overtime costs increase, but her overall productivity could decrease because her employees will spend an increasing amount of their time standing around, waiting for parts.

- Shipping costs could easily double. Motorcycles assembled at the last minute would then have to be shipped overnight in order to meet customer delivery requirements.

There are other things that Lois should consider as well. How much money will she really be saving by switching to this system? Currently she spends approximately $6,400 each year on storage because there is no room inside the plant to keep extra parts. Over the last two years she has taken a loss of $8,000 annually because of parts that she ordered but never used. Eventually the parts were no longer current and Lois was forced to throw them away. Essentially, Lois will conceivably save $14,400 each year by adopting the just-in-time model.

How much could she stand to lose by switching to this model? Lois estimates that each of her customers (local bike shops around the country) provides her with $10,000 of business each year. If she loses only two customers owing to problems with shipping or delays, that loss will negate all of the money she has saved. That does not even take into account the money spent on overtime, shipping, and other unforeseen costs. Is it really worth it for her to switch to this new system? Instead of making such a drastic change, she might simply shop around for cheaper storage. Lois could also have someone come in and conduct better research so that she will not lose quite as much money on obsolete parts.

Manufacturing Cost Justification

The following are things to remember when quantifying manufacturing costs:

- Personnel costs (wages, benefits, recruiting, and initial training)
- Installation and equipment costs
- Training costs (how much time and money will need to be spent training employees on a new system)
- Acquisition costs
- Costs due to delays and down time (shipping costs, overtime)
- Customer satisfaction (loss of customers due to delays in service)
- Operational costs to store, maintain, replace, and replenish

Food Production

Most people who work in purchasing are, unfortunately, slaves to numbers. They are usually none too interested in the relative value of a product or service; they want to know only what will cost them the least. One of my former clients ran a production facility that handled potatoes. This client, I'll call him Smith, would receive several tons of potatoes each week and his equipment would transform those potatoes into french fries, curly fries, and other potato products. Smith needed to purchase some new potato-slicing equipment, so he asked his purchasing agent to gather some proposals and find the best deal. Lou, the purchasing agent, solicited proposals from three companies.

Company A quoted a price of $205,000 for the new equipment and installation. Company B sent in a price of $230,000, and Company C had the lowest bid, at $185,000, for equipment and installation. Lou assumed that all of the products were of relatively equal value and decided to reward the contract to Company C because its price was the lowest. Three months later, after Company C had installed the new product, the potato slicer inexplicably broke. Smith called Company C, but it said its technician could not get there for two days! Meanwhile, Smith's plant was completely shut down.

How much money was Smith losing while he waited for Company C to service his broken machine? His plant averaged 1,000 bags of potatoes each hour, and the bags sold for $2 apiece. This means he was losing $2,000 in revenue each hour; after forty-eight hours that totaled $96,000 down the drain. Looking back, was it worth it for Smith's company to purchase the cheapest equipment (saving $20,000–$45,000)? Obviously not, but how were Smith and Lou to know this unless the salespeople from Company A or Company B pointed it out to them?

As a sales professional you need to provide this type of scenario for any customer worried that your product or service is too expensive. Here are some questions you could ask to do a cost justification in such a situation:

- What is the difference in price between my quote and the least expensive quote?
- How much money does it take each hour to keep your company running? (This would include wages for personnel, electricity, heat, etc.)
- How much money does your company make per hour?
- If this cheaper equipment were to break, how much money would you lose during each hour it took to get it fixed?
- Will this other company guarantee that it will be able to service any broken equipment within an acceptable time frame?
- We want to give you the best price, but we are not willing to sacrifice quality. Has this other company told you how it is able to keep its prices so low?

Food Production Cost Justification

Here are some things to remember when quantifying food production costs:

- Hourly costs (wages, facility costs, and profits per hour)
- Installation and equipment costs

- Quality of service provided by contracting company
- Guarantees of quality or service by contracting company
- Customers lost due to delays in production
- Delivery costs
- Down-time costs
- Reliability of equipment
- Risk and costs of food spoilage
- Operational costs to store, maintain, replace, and replenish

Customer Service/Technical Support

Sometimes we just luck into situations where validating the costs is easy. Another client of mine, Lisa, sells cell phones, pagers, and other telecommunications equipment to companies throughout the United States. She called a national electronics company that employs nearly 3,000 technicians across the United States. The technicians travel from site to site, bringing customers new parts and fixing broken ones. They need to keep in constant contact with the central dispatcher in Memphis, and they need to be able to communicate with one another. Lisa asked Shawn, the vice president of service, if they could discuss new telecommunications equipment. Shawn responded, "That's the last thing we need. Our technicians already have too much equipment!" Then he hung up.

Lisa, startled, wondered what all the fuss was about. She decided to do some investigating on her own and contacted one of the regional managers, Jen. Lisa asked Jen about the state of her technician's cell phones and other communications equipment. Jen responded that her technicians not only had cell phones; they also each carried pagers and two-way handheld radios. Lisa could not believe it! She asked Jen how much money all of this technology cost. Jen thought about it for a minute and said she estimated that the cost for all of these things was about $750 per year for each technician.

Lisa asked Jen if she thought that all of these things were necessary. Jen said, "No, not really. We started with pagers about fifteen years ago, before cell phones were really popular. Then we got cell phones, but we kept the pagers because the technicians needed to be able to get text messages from the home office. Then, the two-way handheld radios came on the market and we purchased those because we didn't have to pay for the minutes that technicians spent talking with each other." Lisa asked Jen, "What if I could offer you a phone with text capability that also had the option for two-way radio use. Would you be interested?" Jen said, "Of course, but I can't make that decision."

After hanging up with Jen, Lisa started calculating numbers in her head. Seven hundred fifty dollars times 3,000 technicians nationwide came to $2.25 million. Lisa could not believe it: This company was spending $2.25 million each year on communications equipment! Lisa's company could provide the same services, in one piece of equipment, for $750,000 each year. Not only would the company save $1.5 million each year, but it would also make things much easier for the technicians. Now they would only have to carry around one cell phone instead of a cell phone, pager, and two-way handheld radio. Lisa once again called Shawn, but this time she had hard numbers to present.

Customer Service/Technical Support Cost Justification

Here are the things to remember when quantifying customer service and technical support costs:

- Overlapping technology (ask about existing technology to get an idea of what the company is currently paying)
- Personnel costs (wages, training, recruitment, and benefits)
- Equipment and operational costs (for technical support this includes office space, phones, and desks, etc.; for customer service that travels—like the example above—costs include trucks, gasoline for the trucks, and technician uniforms, etc.) plus any costs to service, maintain, replace, or upgrade
- Error rates (if technicians or customer service representatives are not well trained the consequences can be dire)
- Customer satisfaction (how much each customer is worth; how many customers the company loses each year due to price issues, poor service, or unnecessary delays)

Using Voice Mail
and E-Mail

It is tough to ask questions by leaving messages on people's voice mail and e-mail, but it is not impossible. One of the best ways to take advantage of these services is to use a variation of the educational question (see Chapter 5).

Using Voice Mail

Here are some great examples of how to provoke a customer response via voice mail:

- "According to *JAMA,* there is a case of pneumonia among ventilator patients every week at busy ICUs, and up to 40 percent of these patients die. Over the last twelve months I have been working with a hospital in northern New Jersey, and during that time not one patient on a ventilator has developed pneumonia. Is this a problem you feel you need to address? If so, please call me at _____ [your phone number]."

- "Hi, my name is _____ and last week I read an article in the *Wall Street Journal* that claimed drug testing is an ineffective tool to weed out poor-quality job applicants. Yet, five times as many companies test for drugs today compared to ten years ago. I have worked with a company in your industry that has reported saving over $5 million by streamlining its hiring process and increasing its retention rates. Is this something you're looking to address? If so, please call me back at _____."

- "The *New England Journal of Medicine* reports that sepsis, a blood infection that afflicts vulnerable patients, kills an average of 42 percent of the people it afflicts. We are working with a number of clinicians who have cut that number in half. Is sepsis a problem in your hospital? Please call me at _____."

- "Hi, my name is _____ and I recently read an article in *U.S. News & World Report* that stated that over 75 percent of high-tech firms today turn to foreign workers to manage their help-desk operations. One of the key challenges seems to be surmounting the language barrier and the difficulty customers have had communicating with the new help-desk personnel. My company is currently working with a client who has addressed this concern and increased customer retention by 30 percent over the past twelve months as a result of our services. Is this an issue you are experiencing? If so, please call me."

Here are some templates to help you form more educational questions to suit your situation. Simply fill in the blanks.

- "Hi, my name is _____ and I recently came across some information that would be of interest to you. While reading the trade journal *X*, I learned that _____. How has your company been affected by this issue? We have some answers. Please call _____."

- "Hi, my name is _____ and I have learned about some pending legislation that might affect your company. The legislation is _____. Does your company have a plan in place to deal with this change? Over _____ [number of companies] in your industry have turned to us for solutions."

- "Hi, my name is _____ and I read an article this morning in _____ that claimed _____. My clients' experiences have been different, however, and I was wondering how your company's experience compares."

Using E-Mail

Here are some examples of how to provoke a customer response via e-mail:

- "I am writing to you because my company has had great success working in the _____ industry. We have been able to increase profitability and bring new products to market at a faster rate. I know that you are extremely busy and not usually keen on listening to sales pitches, so I thought I would let our success speak for itself. Here's the text of a letter of thanks that my company received from Company X [a leader in the field that will inspire trust in the prospective customer] detailing the success it has had thanks to our system. If you are interested in learning more about our services, please contact me at _____."

- "I happened to be reading an article this morning in the *Wall Street Journal* that I thought would be of interest to you. The article quoted an industry insider saying that firms specializing in property and casualty insurance should expect to experience record growth in the next five years. Anyway, I was just wondering if you had seen the article and what you thought about it. We are currently working with a number of firms that are already experiencing double-digit growth. If you have a chance, either drop me a line or give me a call at _____ and I can share some ideas I have with you. Thanks!"

- "Just this morning I read an article in the *Washington Post* that said that employees in large companies spend an average of two hours each day on the Internet for personal reasons. Are you looking for ways to improve productivity? My company's product has helped other large corporations with this type of problem. If you think this is an avenue you would like to pursue, please contact me at _____."

- "I am writing to you because I was reading an article this morning (see attached document) and thought of your company. The article from the *Journal of the American Medical Association* cited a study comparing the sales practices of various drug companies. The study found _____. Is this an issue you are experiencing? We are currently working with numerous pharmaceutical companies, and as a result of our efforts, our clients are reporting on average a 15 percent increase in sales."

- "According to the *Wall Street Journal*, over 225,000 people die every year due to medical errors. We have been working with over 100 hospitals throughout the United States. Over the past twelve months, these hospitals have reported eliminating over 40 percent of errors as a result of using our product. Is this an area that you would like to address? If so, please call _____."

Here are some templates to use in constructing your educational questions for e-mail.

- "I am writing to you because I recently read an article in _____ that I thought would be of interest to you. The article claimed _____. Is this something you are concerned about? If so, we have some answers for you."
- "I have attached an article I thought would be informative for you. The article states _____. I think that this trend/legislation/demographic provides an opportunity for your business. Are you interested in ideas that would take advantage of this opportunity? If you would like to contact me to talk about possible avenues we could pursue, you can reach me at _____."
- "I am writing because my company has had great success with businesses in your industry. I have included the text from a letter by _____, the president of _____. In his letter, he raves about how successful our plans have been. We have saved him over $3 million in the past twelve months. Are you looking to streamline your process in this area? If you are interested in learning more about our services, please contact me at _____."

Seeing the Plan in Action

I HAVE GIVEN YOU a lot of information, and it might be difficult to imagine what a sales call looks like when it incorporates all of the tools presented in this book. Unfortunately, I cannot be there with you to demonstrate my techniques, so I have chosen to do the next best thing. On the following pages you will find a complete scenario of a sales call, from beginning to end and using all of the different types of questions I have introduced. I have chosen to use an example in the medical field because many of my customers tell me that this field grows by leaps and bounds each year, but it is often difficult for a salesperson to get that first foot in the door. If you do not do business in this area, do not worry. I have left out much of the technical jargon in order to focus on the ways in which salespeople can connect with customers. As you read the following example, take note of the various methods employed by the salesperson and the perseverance needed to complete this sale.

Samantha, Our Salesperson

Samantha sells handheld electronic medical devices to hospitals and other patient-care facilities. Samantha's product, MedInfo 2000, allows doctors and nurses to have instant access to a patient's medical records, as well as reference information concerning drug interactions and the latest treatments. The MedInfo 2000 enables hospitals to synchronize patient information, which saves precious time and reduces error rates by as much as 10 percent. The product also gives doctors access to up-to-date medical information that they can use to better treat their patients.

Whereas previous handheld devices were bulky and unreliable, the MedInfo 2000 is lightweight and extremely accurate. Samantha's product also helps to protect patient privacy by eliminating paper records, which can be read by anyone with access to a hospital room. The MedInfo 2000 has password-protected capability that ensures that only authorized personnel can view confidential information.

There are several problems Samantha must overcome in order to complete any sale. One of her biggest problems is the product's complexity. It often takes Samantha several minutes to explain the possibilities of the MedInfo 2000, but by that time most customers have lost interest. Another problem Samantha must face involves the initial expense of her product. The cost to set up the MedInfo 2000 system in an average-size hospital often exceeds $300,000. This money is needed to create a secure computer network that will be accessible throughout the hospital, and to buy handheld devices for hospital staff. Most low-level administrators or purchasing agents react with horror when they hear prices like this, and then Samantha must convince them of the benefits of her system. Once Samantha illustrates the positive aspects of her product, most hospitals agree to the initial expense, but the hardest part of the sale is getting her foot in the door.

Day 1. Samantha Talks with a Manager in Accounting

Today Samantha calls on Greenville Hospital, a medium-size hospital in the suburbs of a large city. Samantha knows that this hospital has been trying to revamp its image and grow its market share, but it has come up against a wall because of the larger-than-life reputations of other nearby hospitals. She hopes that employees of the hospital will view her product as a great opportunity rather than just another expense.

Samantha first calls on a manager in the accounting department who is listed on the hospital's website as a contact. Here is their conversation:

Samantha: Good morning. How are you doing today?

Manager: I'm okay. How can I help you?

Samantha: I am calling to talk with you about a product used by state-of-the-art hospitals around the world. The product is MedInfo 2000. Have you heard of it?

Manager: No, I haven't. What is it?

Samantha: The MedInfo 2000 is a handheld electronic medical device that keeps electronic files for patients and gives doctors and nurses access to reference materials as well as the latest treatments.

Manager: That's interesting, but I bet it is expensive. [Now our salesperson needs to qualify the situation to find out how interested the manager might be.]

Samantha: I know that we all worry about price, but there are times when the benefits outweigh the cost. So that I can better understand your situation, I would like to ask you just a few questions. When the hospital considers a new product, what is the typical evaluation process?

Manager: Well, right now the hospital is not evaluating or approving any new purchases. Over the last three or four years we have seen increasingly smaller profits and so the "powers that be" have proclaimed a moratorium on spending. We just can't do it.

Samantha: Well, thanks so much for your time. I really appreciate it.

Our salesperson realizes from her qualifying question that this person does not have the power to make a purchasing decision at this time. Furthermore, he probably does not have all that much insight into the day-to-day operations at the hospital. She decides that she should not spend her time with these midlevel administrators because they have been intimidated into cutting their spending. Instead, she will focus on the doctors and nurses—the people who would actually be using her product—and hope that they will have enough power to make the hospital executives listen.

Samantha calls the hospital directory and asks for the name and phone number of the head nurse. She is given the information and calls the number but she gets sent directly to voice mail. Knowing that the head nurse probably sifts through dozens of calls each day, Samantha tries her best to be memorable with her message:

Hi, Karin, my name is Samantha Fox, with MedInfo, and I am calling in regard to the fact that nurses spend half their time on administrative functions—time they would rather spend on their patients. Since we've helped over 25,000 nurses reduce their workload on average 40 percent, I'd like to discuss with you how our product could make your life a little easier. If you could call me back when you get a chance, we could discuss this further. My number is 555-555-1212. Thanks!

Although Samantha left only a short message, she piqued Karin's interest. Karin wondered, "Is there really something out there that could make my life less stressful? Gosh, I hope so!" She decides to call Samantha back first thing the next morning.

Day 2. Samantha Talks with the Head Nurse

At 9:00 the next morning, Samantha gets a call from the head nurse, Karin. Unlike the accounting manager she spoke with the day before, Samantha thinks that Karin will not be as focused on budgets and cutting spending. Samantha has learned from her past selling experiences that people in Karin's position are most often concerned about keeping their nurses happy (internal customers) and making sure that the patients are safe (external customers). If she can steer the conversation toward these two areas, Samantha believes she will make an ally in Karin. Here's their conversation:

Karin: Hi, Samantha, this is Karin, the head nurse over at Greenville Hospital. I got a message from you yesterday.

Samantha: Karin, thanks so much for returning my call. As I mentioned yesterday on your voice mail, our company, MedInfo, has empowered more than 25,000 nurses to do what they love doing—providing outstanding patient care, rather than pushing mounds of paperwork. I don't know if what we offer is suitable for your needs but, to find out, may I ask you some questions?

Karin: Yes, go right ahead.

Samantha: Many nursing professionals we work with complain how they spend more than 50 percent of their time on paperwork and record keeping, a problem that was recently highlighted in *U.S. News & World Report.* Did you happen to see the article? Is this an issue that you're trying to address? [Here is a great educational question our salesperson has used to get the conversation started.]

Karin: No, I did not see the article, but, yes, I would have to agree that as nurses we do spend about half of our time on paperwork. It's a ridiculous waste of time! [Our salesperson can tell she hit a hot button by the way the customer responded to the question. Once that happens, the salesperson immediately begins to build rapport with the customer because the customer wants to open up and vent her frustrations.]

Samantha: With all of this time spent on paperwork, do you have concerns about how that affects the care given to patients? [This is a great question that follows up on the customer's statements.]

Karin: I really do. I know my nurses are great at their jobs and extremely dedicated to our patients, but it seems that over the past several years we have become stretched too thin. When I first became a nurse, fifteen years ago, it was typical for a nurse to be responsible for six patients at a time. Now my nurses must care for twelve patients each, and we have more paperwork than ever before! The insurance companies and the new privacy laws mean that each patient has a stack of paperwork traveling with him— paperwork that the nurses have to fill out. My nurses are exhausted and frustrated.

Samantha: It sounds like you probably lose a lot of nurses because of this. I know that the national rate for turnover in nursing is pretty high. How is it for Greenville? [Once again our salesperson just follows the flow of the conversation and asks questions related to topics brought up by the customer.]

Karin: Well, the national average is 15 percent, but for the last two years we have had a 20 percent turnover rate. It is really unfortunate because we have lost some great nurses owing to these long hours and hectic schedules. [Our salesperson has uncovered one motivation for the customer: keeping internal customers, in this case it is nurses, happy.]

Samantha: When you lose nurses like that, is it hard to find replacements?

Karin: Sure it is. There is a nationwide nursing shortage right now, and even when we find new nurses we have to spend several weeks training them on hospital procedures and filling out paperwork. This means that another nurse must take time out from caring for her patients and train this new person.

Samantha: How does this affect the patients? [Here our salesperson is broaching the topic of external customers.]

Karin: My nurses are extremely good at what they do and they give the patients the best care possible. When you are stretched thin as a nurse, however, the best care is not always good enough. It's hard not to feel responsible. As head nurse I am supposed to be the manager and the motivator, but lately I have found it difficult to stay positive. [It is evident that this customer needs something to turn her situation around. It is now finally time for our salesperson to talk about her product.]

Samantha: Well, Karin, I am sure you know there is no magic bullet that will make your problem go away. I do have something, however, that I think will help. My product is the MedInfo 2000, which is a handheld electronic medical device that keeps electronic files for patients and gives doctors and nurses access to reference materials as well as the latest treatments. They are like minicomputers that can communicate between one another as well as store information.

Karin: Well, Samantha your product sounds interesting, but how would it help me?

Samantha: The MedInfo 2000 eliminates 95 percent of all hospital paperwork because it stores patients' files electronically. When a nurse administers medication, for example, instead of having to write down the date, time, type of medication, and amount on a patient's chart, she simply presses a few buttons and it is automatically recorded in an electronic file. Within each hospital, the MedInfo 2000 uses a common network and server so that all of the entries to a patient's chart are updated automatically. This eliminates the risk of a patient's getting a double dose of medication, the wrong dose, or not getting his medication at all. The handheld device also offers nurses and doctors instant up-to-date reference material about drug interactions, correct dosage for specific heights and weights, and the latest treatments. There is also a program that allows the user to enter a patient's symptoms and then view a list of possible diagnoses. Somerville Hospital has been using this technology for the past year and has witnessed dramatic improvements in patient care.

Karin: Wow! You are working with Somerville? You guys must be good. The system you are talking about, even though I am not sure I understand it totally, sounds like it could save my nurses a lot of time and ensure that the patients are safe. You know what? I would really like for you to talk to the doctor's committee about this. They meet every other Wednesday, so they will be meeting tomorrow. If I could set it up, would you be able to come in?

Samantha: Sure, I would love to. What do you think they would be most interested in hearing about? [Our salesperson wants to make sure that she can tailor her information to the specific group with which she is meeting. She also wants to make sure she gets as much inside information as possible about these other decision makers.]

Karin: I think that the doctors would be especially interested in the special functions you talked about—specifically getting the latest information on drug interactions and treatments. Also, most doctors realize how bad their handwriting has become, so I think they would embrace a system that would help eliminate the need for filling out paperwork by hand. Doctors in our hospital also worry about malpractice lawsuits because insurance premiums have gotten so high. Anything that would better insulate them from lawsuits would be a definite plus. [Our salesperson has discovered that these customers focus on external customers as well as personal career goals.]

Samantha: Well, thanks so much, Karin. I will wait for you to contact me and give the specifics for the meeting tomorrow.

Day 3. Samantha Meets with the Doctor's Committee

Karin contacted Samantha to confirm that the doctor's meeting is at noon the following day in the hospital lounge. Although Karin cannot be at the meeting because of a prior commitment, she gave Samantha full reign to share any of the comments and concerns she voiced the day before. Samantha comes to the meeting prepared to do business.

After a few pleasantries are exchanged and she has given a brief introduction and overview of her company, she opens the meeting:

Samantha: I want to thank all of you for agreeing to meet with me. I do not want to take up too much of your time, but I would like to hear about the major issues that concern you. Could you share with me your level of satisfaction with the current patient chart system at Greenville?

Doctor #1: I would say that we are not all that satisfied. Currently we use a combination of computer and paper files, and information from one system often gets lost in the other system. Personally, I hate filling out all of this paperwork because it seems to be redundant and a waste of time. As doctors I think we would all rather be spending more time with the patients, rather than filling out paperwork in triplicate.

[There are murmurs of agreement from the other doctors.]

Doctor #2: Plus, I am afraid that a fatal mistake is going to be made one day. You have so many different people—doctors and nurses, not to mention orderlies—who interact with the patient and I worry that communication breaks down. If I prescribe a medication and tell one nurse, she might be busy and hand it off to another nurse. That is fine and it happens all the time, but what if the second nurse did not hear the instructions correctly and gives the wrong medication or the wrong dosage? I don't want to be liable for that.

[The doctors all nod their heads in agreement.]

Samantha: So, if I am hearing you correctly, you want to have less paperwork to fill out and a better system of communication with other hospital personnel. Well, I can assure you that I have a product that could help. [Samantha goes on to tell the doctors about the MedInfo 2000 and reiterates the benefits she had explained to Karin. The doctors are extremely excited about the possibilities of this new system and after talking with Samantha tell her that she has their wholehearted support. The doctor in charge contacts the hospital president's secretary, who schedules an appointment for Samantha in two days.]

Day 4. Samantha Gathers Information and Research on Issues Relevant to Greenville Hospital

This is the day before her big meeting with the president of Greenville Hospital. Samantha knows that her product could really help this hospital, its staff, and its patients. She knows that the changes brought by the MedInfo 2000 could take Greenville to another level and put it on a par with the other major hospitals in the area, like Somerville.

Samantha decides to organize all of the information she has learned from the nurses, doctors, and even the manager of accounting in order to be fully prepared to meet the president. She catalogs some of the facts and figures she has discovered:

- The nursing staff at the hospital has a 20 percent turnover rate. This is 5 percent higher than the national average.

- There are 500 nurses on staff at the hospital, so this means each year they are losing 100 nurses. According to Karin this is mostly due to the extreme stress and high level of frustration because of disorganization and miscommunication.
- It costs at least $10,000 to recruit and hire a new nurse.
- The doctors fear that miscommunication and poor documentation might lead to more malpractice suits. The hospital is already involved in three lengthy and costly suits and cannot afford any more.
- The error rate at Greenville Hospital, according to public records, is 4 percent, which translates to 20,000 errors per year (the hospital sees 500,000 patients per year).
- Greenville Hospital has one of the lowest insurance reimbursement percentages of any hospital in the country. The Insurance Institute, which keeps records on insurance reimbursement, told Samantha that Greenville receives payment for only 73 percent of its bills because of poor record keeping. Most hospitals nationwide average at least 85 percent reimbursement, and some get as high as 90 percent.

After Samantha talked with Karin and the doctors, she went back to her friend in accounting. (She was careful not to burn bridges even though he had not been able to help her at the outset.) She asked him to estimate how much money each year had to be written off because of improper record keeping. He estimated the loss to be close to $5 million each year.

Day 5. Samantha Sits Down with the President of the Hospital

Samantha knows that she cannot hold back when talking with Diane, the president of the hospital. The MedInfo 2000 could be saving Greenville Hospital millions of dollars each year and ensuring that patients get the best care possible. All Samantha has to do now is convince Diane that the initial investment of $400,000 (Greenville Hospital has no good network to tap into, so the system would have to be created from scratch) is well worth it. Samantha knows that at this level most customers are chiefly concerned with taking the company to the "next level," beating the competition and saving money.

After several minutes of small talk, Samantha gets down to business. She shares with Diane all of the information she has learned over the last week, including the worries of doctors and nurses about patients and the large amount of money lost every year owing to poor record keeping. Diane is impressed with Samantha's ability to gather information and lay it all out on the table. After hearing Samantha's assessment of the hospital's condition, Diana shares her own frustrations. She talks about wanting to make changes but fearing that others in the hospital (like the doctors and nurses) would resist change. Now Diane knows that she and her staff share many of the same concerns, and that the hospital is ripe for an overhaul. Samantha then gives Diane a chance to envision what the future could bring for her and the hospital if all of these problems were solved.

Samantha: If we could eliminate these problems of miscommunication and disorganized paperwork, these problems that are costing you at least $4 million each year, what effects do you think that would have on Greenville? [This vision question can help the customer focus her attention on the benefits of the product to the organization as a whole.]

Diane: If we could do that, then the hospital would be able to acquire the new medical technologies and superstar doctors rather than try to simply make payroll each month.

Samantha: If you could go to the hospital's board of directors and tell them that you have saved the hospital $4 million each year and increased the hospital's standing in the community, what would that mean to you? [This second vision question emphasizes the effects of this change on the customer, rather than the company.]

Diane: I would not have to worry about being replaced by some cutthroat businessperson who was concerned only about money. I am a doctor and practiced medicine for twenty years before taking an administrative position. I know that a hospital cannot excel without great doctors and nurses, but the board of directors has been pressuring me to get rid of some of our best staff because of their high salaries. Now that I can go to them and show them that we will be saving millions of dollars, I think we'll all feel a little more secure in our jobs. [This answer reveals the customer's fear of losing her job and her fear of failure because she is also at risk of losing her staff.]

Samantha: Diane, that is great to hear. In your role, it's important to keep your eye on the big picture. Let's say three years from now, what professional goals would you want to have achieved by then?

Diane: Well, I want to worry less about the hospital's budget, and concentrate more on attracting the most innovative doctors and purchasing the best medical technology that money can buy. In fact, I want Greenville to be the leader that Somerville is now. Also, it would be nice to finally take a vacation after three years without one. Now, let's get started on that contract. . . . [By asking this question our salesperson has helped the customer move beyond her fears and onto her desires. The customer now sees a link between the salesperson and the future success of the company, as well as future success for the customer herself.]

You may be wondering why our salesperson continued to ask vision questions after it was clear that a sale was in the works. It is not enough to go through your business life making single, shortsighted sales. A better strategy is to form relationships, to position yourself as a partner and see the sale through to the end and beyond. The bonding that occurred between Samantha and Diane over Greenville's future and Diane's place in it will translate into loyalty and trust down the road. Besides that, these various questions allow a salesperson to get to the root of a customer's desires. It is only through a real understanding of a customer and her situation that everyone's needs are met. This not only allows for a tailored response at the outset but also ensures that the relationship will endure beyond the signing of contracts.

Index

About the Author

PAUL CHERRY has more than twenty years of experience in sales, management, executive leadership, and performance-improvement strategies. As president and CEO of Performance Based Results, an international sales and leadership training organization, he instructs more than 5,000 sales professionals each year on how they can improve their selling techniques. Paul has worked with 1,200 organizations, ranging in size from Fortune 500 companies, including Johnson & Johnson, Federal Mogul, Medtronic, Moody's, Comcast, Blue Cross, Wells Fargo, Shell Oil, and GlaxoSmithKline, to small and mid-sized businesses, in industries as diverse as healthcare, manufacturing, telecommunications, publishing, financial services, and distribution.